A Mingled Yarn

Jean L. Sealey

Writing about her life.

Edited by Marianne Hulse

Preface

I met Jean soon after I moved to Belper in 1996. I knew no one in the area, and I joined the local writer's group which met in the Red Cross Building in Babbington Hospital.

Jean was one of the writers in the group, and we became friends. I admired her writing and we collaborated in publishing one of her novels, "This Way Out", using the Amazon Create Space. All proceeds from this book were donated to Age UK.

Jean died in 2019 and she left a room full of her writing. I felt privileged to be asked to look at these papers.

Amongst the writings is a memoir Jean wrote between 1981 and 1983 which she titled "A Mingled Yarn". It is a fascinating account and exploration of her life. I would love to have been able to ask her more about it.

I have combined this account with some other pieces of her autobiographical writing to create this book. Although there are some pieces which have duplication I have felt it worthwhile to include them as they have been written by Jean at different times in her life and each one adds just a little more colour to the picture.

I hope you would have been pleased with this book and I was so fortunate to have met you, Jean.

Marianne Hulse.

Contents

A Mingled Yarn

Reflections and Resolutions

Jean Sealey

Written 1981 - 1983

Edited by Marianne Hulse

"Despite periods of tension and misunderstanding which are a normal part of every united family's development, our continued and deepening caring for each other has led to the kind of stability which has made it possible for me to write this book, primarily for them."

A Mingled Yarn - Contents

I

"A Journey in my Head"

On a night in early June 1921 there was, I have been told, a severe thunderstorm in the Chiltern Hills, and between flashes of lightning, I entered this world. More than half a century later another disturbance - this time within myself and quite unconnected with the elements - became the genesis of this book.

Yehudi Menuhin began to write his autobiography "Unfinished Journey" at the age of sixty. He said:

"Once travelled the route is clear, but prescience did not divine it and I am at least, in part accountable for the turns it took."

For me, one of the most feared experiences would be the horror of leaving this world without ever having reached some understanding of why or how I have passed through it, and for several years now I have been contemplating an attempt at an "archaeological self-examination" such as Menuhin achieved in his book. His genius and greatness of character have brought him opportunities and fame far beyond the average. Yet essentially his story is relevant to the most humble and ordinary of us as an account of one person's development and fulfilment, in his case resulting from a true idealism and love of humanity, which I would suggest are as important a part of his personality as his musical genius.

The route I have so far travelled is gradually becoming more clear to me, and because I want to share some of its beauties, its joys, its lessons and its hazards, if only with my family and. friends as readers, I am making an attempt to discover what led me to make that particular decision. To follow this signpost, to accept another metaphorical lift along the way, all of which have brought me to my particular present self. Although it is given to none of us to see the way ahead, perhaps by honest consideration of the past, the future may be more serene, more productive.'

For the first time in nearly forty years I now have leisure and opportunity to consider in greater depth those areas which have for so long had to be relegated to the fringes of my life, and often out of it altogether for some periods. I have resented this, at times unreasonably and angrily. Now I can see that having been granted what I hope may be a time for expansion and exploration, it may have been advantageous often to have had so little choice about my route to the present - I might have missed so much. Choice based on ignorance and inexperience can prove disastrous.

The basis on which I shall try to recall the high roads, lanes, by-ways and paths which have made up my journey so far will be to consider the development of those areas of life which have remained of abiding interest from my childhood through to the present time.

In order to make my purpose clear to myself and to anyone who may wish to read this record with any degree of understanding, it may be helpful to quote here two extracts from some notes I made in preparation for such a book. The first was written in 1976, when I was 55, and reads:

> "Learning to ask questions rather than to accept what is offered by life is perhaps the single most important lesson which should result from our education. It is a lesson which many are never taught and which I am only now beginning to master. The protective coating of received opinions, of apathy or of a decision simply to ride the various waves of experience on which we are

carried through life, provides a fairly effective proof against the distress - pain, even - which accompanies any attempt to face basic facts about the human condition.

I am not a "natural thinker", nor did I ever receive any formal training in logic, argument or debate. In serious discussion between close friends or within the family, the few contributions I make tend to be halting and diffident, however interesting the topic may be to me. Now, late in the day, I am aware that my protective coating has been pierced; I can no longer retreat into apathy or into unthinking agreement with the ideas of other people. I must embark, late though it is, on this journey into self-awareness which may take away some of the nightmare quality of final oblivion.

I have always been slow to recognise the significance of events or situations in relation to myself. It is not until some time after a relationship has existed, or an occurrence has taken place, that its meaning or its effect upon my life becomes apparent. Sadly, this has sometimes been too late, and many opportunities for enrichment or for showing gratitude have been lost forever. In one matter, thankfully, that has not happened; my parents, at eighty-six, are both still alive and well, and I have had the chance to try to indicate to them, however inadequately, something of what I feel for them and what I believe I owe to them."

The second extract, written in the winter of 1980, may give some insight into a state of mind which I believe many women of my generation probably share:

"Wanting to be one's SELF, a person in one's own right, but not being sufficiently self-aware to know how to achieve this...

What has prevented this awareness and subsequent self-fulfilment? It is all too easy to lay the blame at the feet of one's parents, and the need to play the role expected by them whilst one was still financially dependent. Or to suggest that the war prevented a real choice of direction; or that the socially acceptable view of a wife's role in the early 50's was incompatible with total self-realisation; or that the lack of higher education was responsible for stunted intellectual development.

Then in the 1950's we became parents. What conscientious parent does not give absolute priority to their family's well-being? The developing commitments then largely dictated the kind of semi-skilled jobs one could consider taking - jobs which would allow the combination of housekeeping, parenting and wage earning. Any kind of career structure at that time for a part-time housewife without academic qualifications was negligible.

All these factors seem to have combined to produce an encircling barrier well nigh suffocating the little seed of self that has lain at the centre of my life all these years. The shape, size, density and. strength of that barrier has been constantly changing, and there are and have been times when it becomes so thin and fragile that it seems possible to break through it into - what?

A "more complete life"? "True self-realisation"? "A state of being in which one is encountered as a whole person, and not as daughter of, wife of, mother of , secretary to somebody else"?

At other times, that barrier thickens, stiffens, sprouts penetrating inward-facing spikes, develops black holes powered with violent suction, so that whichever way one turns, it seems that the trap is inescapable.

At such times, the tiniest irritations arising from disagreeable household tasks or the most natural interpersonal expectations of others can appear to be the final, life-denying demand which will extinguish forever that tiny seed within.

Could it be that everyone can only exist as a part of other people's lives? - that there is no such being as an independent person?

Even in the course of such speculations I wonder whether an almost total lack of knowledge of basic psychology means that all such ideas are merely nonsensical babblings. If only I knew more - I resent my ignorance... and a voice immediately accuses:

"You can read, can't you? There are books in the house, at the Library?" And I reply; "When can I hope to study or even think undisturbed for long enough or with mental energy enough to begin to make sense of it?"

Is such an excuse rationalisation - isn't it that the role of martyr is an easier one that that of a self-disciplined organiser who can make time to study? Haven't I always refused to let others share enough of the chores because that gives me a martyr's crown, or am I so arrogant that I believe others can't actually do the chores to my liking?

Why isn't there a truly objective judge to whom we could each turn and say:

"Tell us; are we right or wrong in our conclusions?"

I have seen myself as being committed to, say, my job as secretary to nursing administrative staff in a local hospital. Perhaps I have only really been searching for some kind of identity independent of my family, each of whom has strong personalities and very positive, assertive attitudes and achievements. What satisfaction I have achieved by regarding myself as "committed to the job" has eased a little the sense of frustration I have experienced for most of my life.

Hardly ever have I felt that my full mental capabilities or potential have been exercised, and in later years bitterness too is growing, now that what strengths I may have had seem to be waning, just at the time when I might have the opportunity to exercise them."

In the years which have elapsed between the first of those writings and the present time, I think I have matured more than in any comparable period in my life, with the possible exception of the years during which my children were born. Not long after writing as I did in 1976 my mother-in-law, then living alone some 100 miles away, had a fairly serious illness, recovered, gave up her home and at the age of 84 came to live with us.

Within the first six months she had fallen and broken her leg, and spent four months in hospital. She lives with us still, and is now 89. The following year my father died, and this event hit me much harder than I had anticipated it would; he was 88. In the same year, my husband developed a benign brain tumour, necessitating neurosurgery. He has since made a full recovery, but during the period of his operation and convalescence, it was impossible to foresee what the outcome would be. Within a year, my own mother had a stroke, and half-lived for a further three months, finally dying just after her 90th birthday.

During all these events, apart, from odd days' leave taken for funerals and hospital visits, I continued with my job, retiring only on reaching my 60th birthday. Now at last I have the time and opportunity to look back and to try to assess the impact of these happenings and how they have helped to advance me on my journey of self-discovery, and also to consider more deeply those experiences from earlier parts of my life which, from where I now stand., seem significant.

Happily, much of the frustration expressed. in the second outburst quoted above has passed, and I hope that resentment is giving way to a more mature wisdom, so that in whatever time is left to me I can make the optimum use of MY real SELF.

In the 1920's it must have been even less easy for a young woman, married to a man "in business" and gradually prospering, to fulfil herself in ways which have now become more commonplace. I know little of my mother's early life, except for a few anecdotes she recounted over the years which contrasted her childhood with my own. She was one of a family of five brothers and sisters, and spent her first years in south London with her father and a stepmother who, I believe, were equally strict and repressive. Mother however always displayed a quiet breeding and natural intelligence which the circumstances of her life seem to have suppressed. She would have made a wonderful teacher.

Recalling childhood is for me always a happy experience, but only now am I beginning fully to understand why. We were not particularly well-off, although by the time I reached adolescence we were certainly "comfortable". My father, small in stature, and one of a family of eight children, undoubtedly dominated our home. His rare outbursts of temper could terrify my brother and me, but mostly he was kind and-caring, although he left most of our upbringing to Mother in our early days, and was only brought in to discipline us if we had done something which she considered really naughty.

Nevertheless, his presence was always in the background, and I believe now that Mother must often have been torn between what she believed he would wish, and what she herself felt was right in her dealing with us.

I cannot recall ever having been physically punished, although there were occasions when being sent to bed supperless were felt to be a just reward for some major wrongdoing. There was one notable occasion when we, or I, must have been very naughty indeed, since my Mother took most uncharacteristic action to try to impress upon us how much we had upset her. What our offence was I have never been able to recall, though its consequence has recurred to me many times. She packed a suitcase and told us she was leaving us.

The sight of her retreating figure as she walked up the back garden path has haunted me through the years and I can describe it as though it is happening at this very moment. She wears a cloche hat and a dark leather coat, and she walks slowly, the suitcase pulling her left shoulder down a little, and it hangs steady, not swinging at all with her steps. As she reaches the gate, which seems to me already a mile or more away, she pauses, waiting as my shocked silence breaks into howls of distress. My brother is standing behind me and I hear no sound from him. Mother goes through the gate and. closes it.

I cannot see her, for the gate is of solid wood, and high. Sobbing, I run stumbling after her up the path, reach up to click the latch, and there she stands at the other side, waiting. How earnestly I promise her that I will never transgress again! I <u>will</u> be good, always and forever, if only she will stay with us. Somewhere my brother waits, still saying nothing. Perhaps with the superiority of his six extra years he knew all along that it was "only pretend"; perhaps it is only me who has been naughty and I alone have brought this dreadful retribution upon us both. In any event, of course, all ended well, and as far as I remember the event was never referred to again throughout my growing-up.

Strangely, perhaps, I am not aware that it had any deep psychological effect upon my development or our relationships. In fact, almost all of the memories are of a closeness and companionship with my Mother in my gradual discovery of the world. She was able to enter into the small, miraculous domain of a child with the skill of a natural educator and I was allowed to do things and to experiment in ways which must often have tried her patience and added considerably to her daily tasks.

The garden behind our terrace house was long and narrow, and was divided into three main areas. Immediately outside the back door was a covered yard leading to an outside lavatory. Supporting the roof of this area was a latticework of thin laths and there was thus an admirable shelter for the rescued fallen fledglings we brought home to nurse and whose broken legs and wings we tried to mend with matchstick splints, and for the tadpoles, which my brother caught, and which we excitedly watched turning into frogs.

At the end of the main yard was a small patch of soil which "belonged" to my brother and myself, in which we could plant seeds, make mud pies or which we could just neglect, according to our whims. There was also a large, substantial shed containing a stock of firewood, coal, the mangle, a chopping block and other domestic impedimenta. For a period I "lived" here. The floor was made of large rounded bricks, similar to the setts of northern industrial towns, and I spent hours brushing, scrubbing and wiping the crevices between them, and then begging scraps of carpet or matting to cover them. I cleaned the tiny window and hung up a piece of old net, standing a jam jar of wild flowers on the tiny sill. I persuaded Mother to let me take some of my meals in the shed and indeed wanted to sleep there too, but this was not allowed. The pile of coal and wood in the corner spoiled my pride in my first "own home" - I knew they were not part of the contents of a normal living room; but it was a happy haven for me, my dolls and the many familiars who inhabited my world.

In our proper drawing room, inside the house, there was a sofa covered in a strong fabric with a pattern of pink roses on a grey background, the material worn shiny with long use. Here, in the early afternoons when I was very young, Mother would have what she called her "forty winks". I used to curl up into the hollow formed by the angle of her knees and the sofa back and pretend to share her rest period.

I can still recapture the comforting, lived-in smell of that sofa. The need to try to keep still was irksome and I was always on the alert for the first signs that inactivity was coming to an end. I doubt if Mother ever got much rest, but such was her patience that it is the intimacy of that experience which remains vivid rather than any reprimands she may have issued about fidgeting.

A further instance of her loving sympathy with the world of childhood is particularly memorable. I firmly believed in fairies, of course, and on one occasion I asked Mother what were the black smudges inside the base of tulip petals. Without hesitation, she told me that they were the footprints of the tulip fairies who visited the garden when I was asleep. This idea enchanted me. A popular type of seaside greetings card at that time had a flap on the front which opened to release a folded series of tiny photographs of the resort in question. I persuaded Mother to give me one such strip which I cut carefully into its separate pictures and "posted" one into each of about eight tulip blooms before I went to bed. Sure enough, when I went to look in the morning, the fairies had taken them away.

The main garden consisted of a lawn with herbaceous borders and then beyond that and past a high wooden fence there was a patch of no-man's-land common to the five or six houses which made up our terrace. Our portion of this land, which seemed quite extensive to me as a child but which probably measured only about ten by twenty feet at the most, was used for various purposes at different times. For a few years, my Mother kept hens there, and so it had a chicken-wire fence along its outer side and I remember that when the hens had gone I turned it into a ranch and played at cowboys. Where I got the idea from for this unlikely game I don't know, since Western films were no part of my early childhood. Perhaps my brother told me about the Tom Mix adventures he saw on Saturday mornings in the local picture house.

The man from the corner shop a few minutes' walk away used to deliver our groceries once a week, bringing them in a large wicker basket on the front of his bike, using the wooden gate into the back garden. There was a flurry of alarm one day when he was attacked by a rat as he opened the gate and had to be given first aid treatment in our kitchen. Perhaps it was after this that the chickens were got rid of.

There was another very narrow strip of soil immediately under the kitchen window, where year after year I watched the delicate pink shells of the Japanese anemones unfold, and where autumn was heralded by the tiny flames of the montbretia spikes. I had totally forgotten this piece of garden until the last year of my Mother's life, when a clump of these plants in my present garden burst into unusually prolific bloom and I was able to gather a bunch to take to her. She was by then in rapidly failing health, but I hope they were a reminder for her of that old garden of fifty years before.

My schooldays began in a small "kindergarten" run by a kindly teacher and her daughter in a double-fronted house only three doors away from our home. Despite its closeness, I insisted for many months on being taken there and fetched home by Mother - an indication that although 1 have always thought of myself as having been a self-confident child, fear or nervousness must have played a quite considerable part in my make-up.

Perhaps it was something to do with the fact that I had some kind of foot trouble - I had various sorts of treatment to correct flat-footedness and for a long time wore black knee-length boots to strengthen my weak ankles. I found agonising the embarrassment of having to do up thirteen little buttons on each bootleg, with a buttonhook, when I changed into my outdoor clothes before going out to play, or at home-time. The others had generally long left the conservatory where our coats hung, before I was ready.

My brother was six years older than I was, and although there were few serious quarrels between us, we were never very close. His interests were quite alien to me; I felt that he was often embarrassed by me and my childish enthusiasms. I was however, aware from the very first that his schooldays were an almost total misery to him, whereas on the whole I was very contented in my first school. I remember saying as much to him, and feeling helplessly unhappy for him when he responded vehemently,

"Wait until you get to the big school. You won't say the same then"!

I did get to "the big school", a girls' grammar school, via a scholarship examination when I was eleven. This entailed travelling five miles on a bus, a long walk, and staying to dinner. For the first term I was desperately homesick and spent most of my dinner-hours in tears. I was utterly overwhelmed by the size of the building (the Headmistress was also proportionately large and forbidding), by the demands on my intelligence, my physical capabilities, my emotions, and by having to be so self-reliant so suddenly.

By the beginning of the second term, I had to some extent adjusted, and was able to cope reasonably well. I am still not sure whether up to that time I had been spoiled by my parents, or whether a great many children also suffered from the transition to secondary school but showed it less. What I am now convinced of is that the practice of sending children to live away at school at an even earlier age than eleven must result in emotional upheavals for a great many of them, which must indeed be almost impossible to bear. Not least among the factors that had to be faced in the situation were the accepted codes of behaviour, as well as the many formal rules of "the big School".

For those who had taught there for many years, and for the older pupils who had so absorbed the codes by association that they were unaware of them until someone offended against them, I suppose it must have been difficult to comprehend that the newcomer didn't know them by instinct.

That you always stopped and stood still if you passed a member of staff on the stairs. That it was an honour, and not a matter for terrified consternation if your name appeared on the notice board to take part in a lunch-hour hockey trial (even though you had never seen a hockey pitch, much less possessed a hockey-stick!). That you didn't call a fifth-former by her first name when you met her in the corridor, even though your families were on friendly terms and she lived only a street away from you. All the unknown pitfalls, which lay around me at every minute of the day, made those first months at grammar school a time of cold, numb apprehension, and the warmth and familiarity of home became by contrast even dearer. Paradoxically I hadn't the words to explain to my parents why I wasn't happy at that time. I don't think I even knew why. And as time went on, and I made new friends and became involved in the total life of the school, I gradually adjusted - probably the more easily because I rarely questioned all those rules and codes; typically, I accepted and conformed, it seemed the obvious thing to do.

That this response had made life easier was confirmed in my second year when, for the first time in my life, I knew what it vas like to be in really serious trouble, because I broke a rule. Even in doing so, however, I was conforming without question, because it was a rule which everyone else I knew broke all the time.

This rule forbade those of us who travelled on public transport from talking at all during the journeys to and from school. Neither parents nor pupils, nor our friends unconnected with the school, considered that it was either a sensible or a just requirement, but we had been given to understand that it had been formulated because there had been a period of unruly behaviour on public transport by a number of children from both our own and other schools in the area. Thus, it had been felt that if we kept absolutely silent in transit, we could not indulge in unladylike behaviour which would draw the criticism of the public upon the school.

That this theory was patently absurd was demonstrated by the fact that we didn't need to talk to be guilty of ungenteel behaviour; some giggled, sang, or threw books, lunch-bags and other missiles, all of which might have been avoided had we been permitted to talk. In the end, of course, the nospeaking rule was kept by scarcely anyone at any time. But the teachers had for a long while no inkling of this, because - the most absurd aspect of a totally absurd situation - we were all required at each fortnightly form meeting to avow individually in front of our form-teacher and form-mates, that during the past two weeks we had "not talked on the bus/train".

Inevitably, the show-down had to come. The storm burst when the boyfriend of one of the older girls travelled with her one day, they were teased by a number of the younger travellers, and she "sneaked" on the whole lot of us for revenge. (Angela Brazil, where art thou now?)

The period which followed was bizarre in the extreme. Each of us had an interview with the Headmistress, alone. Comparing notes afterward, we found that release from that ordeal came only when we dissolved into tears, were offered a piece of stockinette rag with which to wipe them away, and an understanding was arrived at that to have confessed had made us bigger characters who might one day, with perseverance and a striving towards complete honesty in all things, merit the reward of serving the school as prefects! We were required to promise to tell our parents that we had consistently lied, time after time, but had seen the error of our ways and had now reformed.

We thought it was all over, but worse was to follow. We were ostracised by some of the staff and virtually sent to Coventry by some of our peers - mostly those who never travelled on public transport. I remember in particular one teacher for whom I had up to that time had some admiration and affection, who completely broke my faith in her humanity. My Mother wished me to give her a message about some gift for the pending Summer Garden Fete for school funds. As I approached her desk to give her this message, she looked away from me and said, "Sit down. I don't wish to have anything to do with LIARS." I was devastated, and even at that age was able to apprehend how little understanding she must have had of the essence of childhood innocence. Indeed, I think she contributed in no small measure to the destruction of my innocence because despite my record of "consistent lying", I believe I had been until then wholly without deliberate wrong intent.

My later years at school passed fairly happily. I made the usual passionate friendships which in adolescence rise suddenly to absorb all one's emotional energies, and as rapidly fade into disillusion. There were a few tentative and wholly theoretical excursions into the mysterious world of sex, about which most of us in the thirties were incredibly naïve by comparison with today's teenagers. At that time, the years of an individual's life from 12 to 20 were simply another stage of existence. We were not classed as "teenagers"; we were not a target for commercial or political pressures; and perhaps on the whole a larger proportion of us had an easier transition from childhood to adulthood than young people do today.

Leisure time was almost totally occupied by events connected with the Methodist Chapel and its activities. I fell in and out of love with parsons' sons as they came and went, and with members of the Wesley Guild, the nearest equivalent of which today would be a church youth club, although the age range and types of activity were, I think, wider in our day. This too had its codes and aspirations. In fact, on reflection my growing-up had been encompassed by such tenets, either overt or implied.

Little wonder that I became for so long such an avid acceptor. The School creed, for example, pinned up inside everyone's desk to be noted every time we opened the lid, read, "Our

School tradition of loyalty, hard work and honesty has been worthily won. Let us pass it on unsoiled." Similarly, the code of the Wesley Guild was framed and hung in the large meeting room, exhorting us to industry, clean living, good fellowship and charitable thoughts and deeds.

We were not totally without humour however, and early in our school careers we thought it smartly funny, particularly when we had been reprimanded by a member of staff , to misinterpret the School Motto, "ubi semen, ibi messi" into "You be the servant, I'll be the missus"

The thirties was the heyday of rambles and hikes, and the members of the Guild were nothing if not energetic. Most Bank Holidays saw us setting off on twenty-mile walks, occasions which I remember with much happiness. We discussed many topics and if we were a little earnest in our preoccupation with moral issues, at least we were trying to find some answers to serious questions. At the same time we found real if simple and unsophisticated joy in exploring the countryside and in the campfire songs at the end of the day's exertions. These hikes also provided opportunities for boy-girl relationships to expand. A whole day in one another's company was a rare chance to try out the deeper implications of a possible serious relationship.

All in all, then, these were relatively unremarkable early years; a field of well-rooted but quite ordinary grass, over which the eye might pass noting little to disturb or to arouse expectations or evoke comment. Few fields, however, are without the potential, be it ever so tiny, of some colourful flowerings here and there, which will claim their place amid the uniform blades of green. The delight in words, the balm of music, the excitement of developing knowledge, the challenge of the social environment and the mysteries of personal relationships - these were the seeds scattered through my particular pasture. The development of each of them over the years, sometimes in spurts of growth, sometimes dormant for so long that I was almost unaware of their presence, will form the background against which I look for myself.

II

"Better than Bad Strokes"

The facility with which both my son and my daughter are able to use the spoken and written word is to me a source of pride, albeit tinged with envy. I rejoice in their abilities with language and wish I too were able to argue and discuss matters of importance in so clear and precise a way. I acknowledge that a major part of my weakness here is a failure to think logically and exactly, rather than any deficiency in vocabulary.

Words have always interested me, although any organised study I have undertaken in this area has been of the most meagre and superficial kind. Opportunities have either been missed, or have not arisen. The decision to embark on this present undertaking may well have been dictated by an intent to expunge yet another "if only..." from the record.

What early influences direct our interests? As far as I am aware, the environment of my first years was average as far as written and spoken language was concerned, although certainly in the grammar school we had the benefit of a remarkably sound language education. Not only was the English teaching of a high standard, but the other encouragements such as good drama productions and form and school magazines all paid meticulous, if conventional attention to most aspects of self-expression in words; - not merely correct spelling and grammar, but imaginative interpretation and creativeness.

Many people claim, for example, that Shakespeare was ruined for them by their school "Eng. Lit." lessons. The opposite was true for me and I relished every moment of the reading, analysis, comment, classroom acting and essays in the syllabus. For me the Magician's spell was active from the very first, and it has never been broken. I am sure a major reason for this was the way I was introduced to Shakespeare and other literary giants, by our English teachers.

In earlier days my parents taught us nursery rhymes and poems, my Mother used occasionally to recite at concerts, there were always some books around, and we often played word-games. My Father had wanted to teach and had indeed begun his working life as a pupil teacher, but for some reason had been unable to go on to complete training. His interest in education remained however, and although in later life I recognised it as being relatively uninformed and narrow, he probably contributed in no small way to the development of my own pleasure in words.

Foreign languages also attracted me. At my first school we were taught some French in a very rudimentary way, and with excruciating pronunciation mnemonics; for example "cinque" was prompted by "what the ship did" (sank) and "huit" by "you and me" (we)! Nevertheless, this introduction took away the strangeness from our first French lessons at secondary school. In our third year there, we had the choice of studying a further language or taking Domestic Science at School Certificate level. Having little skill at sewing, and having learned simple cooking at home, I chose to "do" German. We also had one year's work in Latin, which I found difficult and was able to drop. This I have since regretted, as I soon discovered how greatly a sound knowledge of the tongue would have added to my appreciation of English and other languages.

During the fourth and fifth years, we began to think about what would follow our school lives. At that time (the late thirties), higher education was strictly limited, particularly for girls, to the very high fliers. Only a handful of pupils from an average provincial girls' school would stay on beyond sixteen to take Higher School Certificate - the equivalent of today's 'A' Levels - and of these, only a tiny percentage would even consider going to University. Having achieved tolerably good results in most of my School Certificate subjects, I decided to stay on for a further term. This resolve was determined not by the wish to take more examinations or study, but solely in order to take part in the annual school play at Christmas, and during the term I had to decide on some kind of career.

Possibly those few months of 1937 hold one important, if accidental, clue in my current search for self-understanding. I had always been enthusiastic about acting, and had entered numerous festivals, been in school and chapel plays and concerts. (It was called "Elocution" then.) So it seemed perfectly normal to extend my school life by three months simply to play Bottom in Shakespeare's "Dream".

But of course, and here is the clue, one had to do something during lesson periods, and my favourite subject always having been English and language generally, I concentrated on this and vaguely thought of "going into" journalism or publishing. There were no Careers Officers then, and the only advice available for most of us was from parents or one or two helpful teachers, or "contacts" if you were lucky.

I spent most of that last term studying the literary styles of national and local newspapers, learning how to "précis" with some accuracy, mastering shorthand and typewriting, and looking around for some outlet in which to practise the very elementary skills I was thus acquiring. I heard about a small "Free Press" which appeared weekly in a neighbouring town and wrote for information, was given an interview and eventually offered a job at 10/- per week (50p) as the junior in a team of three who produced the paper.

So in early 1938 I joined the H------- Free Press - a journal of a type I had never met before and I imagine there are now few in existence quite like it. It was owned and managed by a Territorial Army Major as a side-line to his printing works in a nearby city. It was staffed by the editor who was formerly a reporter on an orthodox established local weekly, a married part-time compiler of the woman's column, and myself. Distributed free to every household in the area, its costs were met solely by advertisements but unlike today's "Trader" weeklies, our paper carried a large body of editorial matter, both news and comment on local affairs. It was popular and widely read.

At first, I was very much the office junior, sorting advertisements, checking copy and doing general odd jobs and errands, but the editor was an amiable and kindly man who certainly didn't appropriate all the most interesting stories to be covered. It wasn't long before I was out and about in the town (actually little more than a rambling village at that time) collecting news and views for my own stories. I was extremely proud of my first printed paragraphs, and soon became aware of the special kind of relationship with the public, which gives the journalist such a unique responsibility in the practice of his craft.

Naturally, on such a very minor publication this factor hardly kept me awake at night, but the principle is the same whether applied to the tiniest monthly parish magazine or the largest national daily. Words have great power, and an irresponsible or biased account read by even a very few individuals can be hurtful, mischievous or extremely damaging to the society immediately affected by it. This truth, which I discovered at the tender age of 17, has become ever more vividly demonstrated with the rapid increase in mass communication until today it has become one of the most important factors in the immense problems confronting western society.

I had many interesting, amusing and instructive encounters during the short period I worked for the Free Press. I found the frailties and the greatnesses of human beings equally fascinating. At one very grand house, for example, where I had been sent to obtain details of arrangements for a forthcoming charity Garden Party, I was peremptorily directed away from the front door to the servants' entrance at the back. Here I went into the kitchens where a maid was taking a plate from an oven, with two sausages and two potatoes on it. I hastened to apologise for interrupting what I assumed was her lunch. "Oh, this isn't mine", she said. "It's for the master and. mistress. They always eat like this when they're on their own, so they can afford to put on a grand table when they entertain".

Occasionally there were events to be covered which had a measure of importance which went beyond the parochial village-pump reportage. A senior member of the Government of the time lived in the area, and I reported on a policy speech which he made locally. I was very flattered when, having vetted the draft of my report, he said it was the most accurate account of the three submitted to him by the local papers.

On another occasion the then Duke of Kent spoke at the opening of a new Agricultural Research establishment and on being detailed to attend and report the event, I really felt I had "arrived".

However, doubts began to arise in my mind about a career in journalism when I was sent to get a story from a family who had been tragically and rather sensationally (By this quiet town's standards) bereaved. The insensitivity of the notion that a stranger had any right whatsoever to intrude into such a situation caused me to question whether I wanted a life in which that kind of callousness would have to be a necessary quality if one were to succeed. I did not have to make the decision - it was made for me.

In 1938 one of my assignments had been to report on the opening of the new public hall. The ceremony was interrupted by an announcement of Chamberlain's return from Munich carrying the famous piece of paper. In September of 1939 one of the last things I remember happening at the Free Press was that I was sitting in the little courtyard outside the office having a sandwich lunch and I heard the radio news that German bombers had raided Poland. Within a very short time the Major who owned the paper had gone to war, the paper was closed and with its passing went any career I might have had in journalism.

At about this time I was beginning to recognise that some form of further study would be both advantageous for me and also be a satisfying way of using some of my leisure time. I would have liked to study for an external degree in either English or another language, and since in those days very little information or advice on such matters was available once you had left school I sought help from the one person I thought might be well qualified to provide me with some relevant counselling - the Methodist minister.

To this day, I feel a certain resentment for what followed, and wonder how differently my working life and my personal development might have evolved had I not been influenced by him. He was obviously aware of my enthusiasm for study, knew me as a committed and active Methodist, and persuaded me that the right course (in more than one sense) for me would be to study for the Local Preachers' examination rather than for a degree.

I was young, impressionable and respectful of all authority, and I followed his advice. I became immersed in Old and New Testament Studies, read most of Wesley's Sermons together with the prescribed books on Christian Doctrine, and eighteen months, two exams and Trial Sermon later, became an accredited Local Preacher, taking services and preaching in Chapels in the local circuit and also conducting some open-air meetings in parks in the neighbourhood.

I am sure that there was in me then a considerable element of the arrogance, self-righteousness and exhibitionism which I now regard with some suspicion in others who pursue these activities. However, in mitigation I still believe that in the social climate of the late thirties I was sincere in my attitude that the Methodist Church had a contribution to make to society. The doubts and eventual rejection of its beliefs were yet to come.

One thing I certainly now question is the right and wisdom of that particular man, to whom I went for advice, to steer me away from my original intention. It is difficult not to see his action as exploitation of my pliancy to further the Church's good rather than to aid my personal development. I am sure he would have been able to justify himself, with all the might of true Christian objectives behind him. He is probably long dead, but even now I cannot find it easy to forgive him.

Following the outbreak of war in September 1939, the plans for our individual futures which had been taken for granted by me, my family and friends - and presumably by the majority of our fellow-citizens - were shown to be as fragile as eggshells, and when normality was shattered, all our lives spilled messily out.

From the moment the first air-raid sirens sounded, through call-ups, bombings, designation of reserved occupations, blackouts, rationing, maiming, death and all the myriad other effects of total war, everyone's life was affected to greater or lesser degree.

As history reveals more and more details of the weightier issues involved in that conflict, and as the cataclysmic effects on European countries and on the Jewish race in particular continue to influence the histories of whole communities; the immediate consequences for many of us in Britain, as individuals, may now be seen to be comparatively insignificant. But all of our dreams, our intentions, were at the very least suspended for six years, and for those of us just entering adulthood, the adjustments we had to make varied from the trivial to the (sometimes literally) deadly serious.

With the closure of the Free Press I looked for some occupation directly connected with the war effort, and applied for a job with the Ministry of Food which was then recruiting people to help with the enormously complicated administration of the food-rationing scheme. I was accepted, but not having the remotest applicable qualifications for administration, was drafted to a junior audit clerk's post in a local accountancy firm so that an experienced auditor accountant could be released for the more exacting and important task of implementing the scheme.

From my first day in that job I acquired a painful and lasting understanding of what it feels like to be a square peg in a round hole. Not only had I never been confident or accomplished with figures - I didn't even begin to understand the basic principles of bookkeeping. Consequently, in the adjustment to wartime conditions then being made by all institutions, the firm's bosses were obviously not going to let a mathematically incompetent 18-year-old loose on anything more important than the simplest checking of column after boring, repetitive, column of figures. I stuck at it only by persuading myself that in some miniscule and incomprehensible way I might perhaps be helping Britain and the other defenders of the free world to survive. I enjoyed the company of the other non-professional members of staff ; they too had found themselves to be fish not only out of water but grounded, so to speak, on totally alien land into the bargain.

Those few qualified auditors still in post and not released by our recruitment for more vital war work kept themselves very much apart in separate offices, and I can now remember none of their names or faces - with one exception. A kindly young lad who was medically unfit for active service, and physically not very attractive, took a fancy to me and for a few brief weeks we "kept company".

We went to the cinema two or three times, he came once to my home for tea, and he took me to meet his blind mother with whom he lived alone and for whom he cared without other help. I felt sorry for him; admired his devotion to his mother, was grateful to him for proving that audit clerks and accountants, contrary to my belief at the time, were capable of normal human emotions. But we had little in common and the relationship ended as soon as I left the firm, and that came about in this way.

All ideas of a literary-orientated career having been temporarily abandoned, I nevertheless knew that an audit clerk's job was good neither for me nor for the war effort. It so happened that I had a friend, the daughter of our Methodist minister (he of the degree study course debacle),who was due to move on with her family to another Circuit, her father having completed his allotted span with our Chapel. She was at that time employed as secretary to the Chief Engineer of a large local factory which was part of the General Motors Group and by then fully engaged on war production work. She suggested that I apply for her job, and with much misgiving, I did.

I had learned basic shorthand and typing in my last few months at school and had, of course, used both skills whilst working on the Free Press, but my speeds fell far short of those required of an efficient secretary, and I had no knowledge of any form of engineering technology.

However, I got the job and for the first few weeks used to take home my shorthand notebook every night and try to make sense of the hurriedly scribbled, very inaccurate outlines which supposedly represented coherent correspondence and reports about oil filters, diaphragms, plugs and other mysteries, which had been dictated to me a few hours earlier by my very knowledgeable and articulate boss.

Eventually familiarity and practice rescued me and I became, I think, a reasonably useful employee. I enjoyed the job, I liked and respected my boss and his assistant, and for over a year this was the main background of my war on the job front. The Engineer was also the Captain of the factory's Home Guard platoon, and although "Dad's Army" is now synonymous with gently malicious comedy, to us then it was part of the business of survival and we all took our duties seriously. I "clerked" for the platoon and acted as runner for many of the regular battle exercises.

Little scope for creative literary activities arose in any of these areas, but in our spare time, a small group of friends and myself formed a modest little magazine and met regularly to read, listen to and criticise each other's stories, poems and essays. One of that group subsequently married into the aristocracy and has published her own autobiography in which she has recalled some of those meetings and literary attempts. Another friend whose children's stories I then much admired is, I believe, now returning to creative writing after many years of a busy life which gave her, like me little opportunity to practise the craft.

As the war went on, I began to feel that my part in it was still not as direct as it might be. My pre-war pacifism had given place to a conviction that Fascism had to be actively opposed if Europe were not to be bludgeoned into an obscene travesty of what human life was meant to be. I decided to try to join up.

The WRENS was my first choice, I suppose because I was still naïve enough to be tempted by the reported glamour of attachment to the Senior Service, and in any case, I had always been a little romantic about the sea. Disillusionment came swiftly and emphatically as the British class system manifested itself in a manner that brooked no questioning. At my first enquiry the fact that I had no close relatives already in the Royal Navy, no aristocratic connections, and had had only a secondary grammar school education, decisively excluded me from even preliminary consideration.

Next in line was the WRAF. Since my boyfriend at the time (who subsequently became my husband, but that's another part of the story) was by then training to be a pilot, I felt, quite illogically, that we would somehow be closer, despite all the separations caused by the war, if we were wearing the same coloured uniform. Alas, all that the WRAF were prepared to suggest was a shorthand-typist's job, and I wanted a change. (Was patriotism not enough?) After all, if I were going to remain a typist, why exchange a comfortable home and a relatively well-paid and interesting civilian war-work occupation for the unknown discomforts of similar work in uniform, and on a comparative pittance?

So, on my next visit to London I went to the ATS recruiting HQ and was taken round an exhibition depicting the life of the girls in khaki. This included photographs showing the various trades practised by "female soldiers", - cooking, driving, anti-aircraft battery duties and of course the inevitable clerical jobs. The exhibition also included a complete display of all the regulation clothing issue and I both quailed and giggled inwardly at the sight of the voluminous khaki bloomers, thick greenish lisle stockings and heavy footwear which would be part of my everyday dress if I "got in".

During an informal interview with one of the recruiting officers, the phrase "military intelligence" was used, and it became apparent that should I consider applying for work in that area I might not be wasting my time.

As so often in later life, I look back in astonishment at my utter ignorance and innocence in this, as in so many other spheres of life at that time. I had no idea at all what the Intelligence Corps did, but decided to find out more. There duly followed what seemed to me a most impressive and exciting interview somewhere in the underground depths of Whitehall. I recall that my tastes in music (Bach obviously scored a hit), an interest in crossword puzzles and various other seemingly unrelated topics were discussed, and some time later, I was notified that my interview had been successful. The War Office wanted my help to win the war!

Now began a bureaucratic battle, since it transpired that secretarial work for the Chief Engineer was officially classed as "essential war work" and I couldn't be released to join the ATS. What a transformation in status from my days as an inefficient and unwilling audit clerk, working on columns of figures in tradesmen's ledgers smelling evilly of stale fish or stained with blood from the butcher's shop!

Weeks passed, letters came and went between this and that Department of State and myself. Eventually, after what seemed to be complications out of all proportion to the recruitment of so totally unimportant an individual as myself, I was enlisted into the ATS in September 1943 at St. Albans.

I then went to camp in Guildford, Surrey, for the initial square-bashing course. This was reduced to a minimum for those of us destined for the Intelligence Corps, much to the disgust and envy of our fellow recruits. I disliked the military discipline and found it difficult at first to adapt to living so publicly; but I was young enough and sufficiently conditioned by the wartime atmosphere and ethos to find the adventure, excitement and a widening of personal horizons more than compensatory for any negative reactions.

Initial training over, we spent a period of technical training in London, during which time we were on the fringe of one or two bombing attacks and I understood for the first time what real physical fear was. The training was concerned with radio communications - and even then, I didn't fully appreciate what sort of organisation I had joined. The course ended, we were given our postings - some to go overseas, some to remain in London, and I with the majority of the course reported to Bletchley Park.

It still seems odd that now one can say one worked at Bletchley Park during the war, and many people will know that you were part of a huge code-breaking machine. Then, and for thirty years afterwards, we were bound by the Official Secrets Act and had sworn never to divulge anything of what we saw, heard or did in that mysterious and exciting establishment.

Security was absolute, and even between one section and another, one room in a hut and the room next door, no gossip about the work was exchanged, at least among any of the rank levels at which most of us there operated.

I very soon realised that because of the character of the place and the personnel employed in it this was to be, in part, my personal substitute for the University experience I had not had. Every nationality of the Allied Forces was represented, as were most kinds of civilian occupation and all from many different social and economic categories. It was a stimulating environment to find myself in, and apart from the actual work (I never aspired to anything grander than a humble log reader during my whole time there) there were opportunities for every kind of leisure activity. Societies flourished for drama, music, art, sport, chess, boating, dancing - you name it, somebody did it, and many groups included acknowledged experts among their number. The mix of cultures from the different nationalities added to the interest, and I revelled in it all.

At this distance in time, it seems that in addition to the fact that we were undoubtedly sheltered from the war in a physical sense, we were also cocooned from its effects in less obvious ways. The Park was a totally self-contained community, whose citizens enjoyed many and significant privileges denied to those in combat, or to the civilians enduring wartime hardships and dangers on "the home front".

Of course our rations were the same as for the remainder of the population; we lived in bleak Nissen huts; we ate communally; and I suppose we were as vulnerable to air attack as any other area except the obvious targets of large cities and industrial centres. But there was an atmosphere throughout the camp of a life apart from the battle, at times a tranquillity, in which it was possible to pursue personal interests, to develop friendships. To continue in fact to grow in all kinds of knowledge and experience in a way which could not have been possible for so many of our fellow countrymen and women during those years.

Many of my memories of Bletchley confirm this, but perhaps one instance will serve to illustrate what I mean. The basic work, of course, was continuous and we were on duty in shifts throughout the 24 hours, including a long night shift which lasted, if I remember correctly, from midnight to 8 a.m. with a meal break. On more than one occasion some of us, having had our "midnight feast" (the food on this shift always seemed more imaginatively prepared than the daytime Mess offerings), would take out a rowing boat onto the large ornamental lake in the Park grounds. We would drift around in the moonlight, disturbing the flock of Chinese geese and setting them honking across the water.

Conversations ranged over many topics, and the war - at least for the span of those brief hours - seemed a bizarre fantasy, less real and important than, say, the choice of a significant work for the next Drama Group production; the need for a genuine spiritual vocation if one was to enter the Anglican ministry (as one of our number was contemplating on demobilisation); the ethics of marital fidelity; the philosophy of Christian Science (there was an active C.S. community in the Camp); political issues - all this and much more was exhaustively discussed with as much earnestness as on any University campus.

There were many people at Bletchley with considerable academic qualifications or potential in many fields. The opportunity for all of us, particularly those hundreds who would normally never have known such encounters in their peacetime lives, was unique. Rank and class, whether military, social or educational rarely obtruded and I am certain that the experience of the social mixing in that place, at that time, was of enormous benefit to those who were there, and possibly also to many with whom they became involved afterwards in post-war Britain and elsewhere.

By 1945 we were so thoroughly adjusted to wartime living that peace came as a strange, but obviously welcome upheaval. Bletchley Park began to disperse many of its occupants into other areas of the Services to await demobilisation. I was moved to Nottingham to mark time in an Army Post Office unit. It was back to daily square-bashing and a rather dreary routine, enlivened for me first by a course held at Helbeck Abbey to reintroduce us to civilian life (I revised shorthand. and typing, and flirted briefly with the mysteries of Company Law); and later, and infinitely more significantly, by my plans to get married. Women in the Services at that time were released on marriage and for me this happened in June 1946.

We began married life in London, and I got a full-time secretary's job in the head offices of W. H. Smith's, overlooking the Thames near Lambeth Bridge. I can see now that this was in fact a further straining towards some kind of renewed connection with things literary but in fact, as it turned out, it could have been a secretary's job in any other kind of enterprise. The work itself was moderately interesting and conditions and pay were reasonable; the man I worked for certainly was not. He had worked his way up from being a paper boy at eleven, to holding a responsible managerial post in the organisation, and hardly a day passed when he did not parade this fact to his office staff, either overtly or by implication, or in his boorish behaviour. We did not get on!

In the lunch hours I enjoyed exploring the street market and the part of Lambeth which lay behind the Embankment, and the bus journeys across London to and from our flat in West Hampstead were always interesting.

Life for us in post-war London, on a shoestring budget (my husband was on a teacher training course and his grant barely paid the rent of our flat) was exciting, optimistic, entertaining, instructive.

I left Smith's and after a few months in an export-import

agency managed by a gentle Jewish refugee from Germany, decided to take a gamble as a free-lance typist. It was a precarious venture economically, but as an experience it was rich indeed. I typed theses for higher degree students, reports and lectures for psycho-analysts, the manuscript of an appallingly bad novel, scripts for film-makers, letters for fruit importers, a column for a newspaper astrologist - in fact I got a glimpse into a wide variety of worlds. I once even visited the Dorchester Hotel to do some letters for a visiting Australian, and was incidentally treated to a replay of my voice on his new toy - a portable tape recorder, which at that time in this country was a kind of magic box.

Alas, there was little furthering of direct literary accomplishments in this period, and earning enough to keep us in food and warmth was the priority, but encountering such a wide range of personalities once again increased my awareness of people as being infinitely interesting. Now, 35 years on, I realise that those brief acquaintanceships, as in the case of the more developed relationships I experienced at Bletchley, increased my belief in the importance of communication between groups and between individuals.

I did achieve one small literary success in 1949, when I submitted an article on "Music and the Adolescent" to the rather prestigious journal "Music and Letters", edited at that time by Eric Blom. To my surprise it was accepted, and appeared in the issue of January 1949. This was a boost for my self-confidence and I thought that perhaps writing as a career, even if only part-time and home-based, was a possibility for me.

On completion of my husband's training, we moved from London to Leeds, and for two or three years I worked at the University Institute of Education - again in a secretarial role, and there were occasional opportunities for activities not confined to shorthand and typing.

In 1951 our first child was born, and from then until 1981, apart from the occasional poem, or a letter to the newspapers, creative writing stopped. It would seem however that the impulse to set down words to be read - even if only by myself - is still there.

Had I, for any reason, not been available to cook, clean, shop and otherwise care for my immediate family or to type letters for whomever I was employed by at the time, someone else would doubtless have been found to do those tasks. Only I however, can express my particular self and my individual responses to what life has presented to me. So I feel compelled to increase my own awareness and as I do so, if I am not to be totally isolated as a creature I must try to tell others what that awareness shows me.

The stereotyped images, influences, ideas, exhortations hammered at us by television, newspapers, political bodies, religious institutions, even educational establishments, are no kind of substitute for the immediacy and potency of direct interchanges between people with divergent backgrounds, views and aspirations.

Once again communication - real, basic, sincere, significant communication - suggests itself as one possible answer to the "how" of my original question; and of course words are not the only means of expressing to others our ideas and intentions. Beyond the obvious channels of all the art forms there are to be found many other ways of access to one another, if we have but the will and the imagination to seek them out.

III

<u>"Marvellous Sweet Music"</u>

Having no executant ability in music is a source of some regret to me. However, from as early as I can recall, some kind of music has been part of my environment in varying degrees of importance, and of late its contribution to my life has been immeasurable.

In the pre-television age of my childhood, amateur music-making was a normal activity for a large number of people. Pianos were common in many homes; church or chapel choirs and concerts were part of our growing-up; local musical societies flourished; and performing in one way or another, even inexpertly, was taken for granted in many families. It is a joy to observe that some of these activities seem to be returning, although I have the impression that there is now more of a class bias than there was in my childhood.

My parents both belonged to the chapel choir and to the amateur operatic society; both could play the piano from sight, though not to any recognised standard; and both sang as soloists in local concerts. There was also in the house a mandolin. How this exotic instrument came to us I have no idea, but Mother was able to coax quite recognisable music from it. Unhappily, I do not know where it is now.

My brother took piano lessons for some years, and later played drums and saxophone in amateur dance and concert orchestras. He has continued with his musical activities to the present time. I, alas, did not persist with music lessons. I found after my first day at school that I could pick out by ear on the piano the melody of the hymn we had sung that morning, and that was my downfall as far as playing from music was concerned. I lacked the patience to persevere in trying to master the printed score, when I could so much more quickly achieve out of my head even a poor approximation of the notes required. My brother was most impressed by this questionable ability, and when he formed a small dance band in his teens, I occasionally deputised for a missing pianist at open-air concerts for which he was booked - and on one memorable occasion, I stood in for the drummer! -

I loved to attend the light operas in which my parents took part - sometimes it was Gilbert and Sullivan, and I also remember that a production of "Veronique" was a special pleasure because of the Swing Song and of the appearance on stage of a real live donkey. My father was a bass baritone and my Mother a contralto, and they often sang duets both at home and in public. Despite the fact that I can now appreciate that much of the music they sang was light-weight and sentimental, I am nevertheless still affected by nostalgia when I hear, say, "Little Grey Home in the West" or "My Ain Folk". Although not great music, such songs were popular ballads of the time and they reached the hearts of many of their hearers. In their own way they helped to start me along one track towards a wider musical experience.

Other highlights of our childhood years were the annual oratorios produced at the Chapel. Months of choir rehearsals led up to these winter events and the Chapel was always filled to capacity "on the night".

Often, nationally famous soloists were engaged, and although I have now forgotten many of them, I do recall two singers for totally different reasons. Elsie Suddaby because of her uniquely delicate voice, and a male soloist (whose name I cannot recall) because of an incident which probably only a child would notice sufficiently to remember after more than fifty years. This singer was being entertained at our home for the hour or so between his arrival and the performance. I was very young, and fascinated by this celebrity who seemed to a small girl to be a gentle white-haired giant. He refused all refreshment before singing, requesting only a raw egg in a glass. As I watched in amazement, he swallowed this whole and I stood there waiting for him to be sick. Of his singing, I remember very little....

When I became old enough to join the Chapel choir I occasionally took part in the oratorios as well as in the concerts arranged by the organist/choirmaster, and I suppose this was my first introduction to anything approaching classical music. "Elijah", "The Creation" and, of course, "Messiah" were familiar ground, but the scores of such works as "Mount of Olives" and Stainer's "Crucifixion" were there to be studied, if only I had had the motivation or the initiative to have done so, - but I didn't.

Music at school I remember as being only sketchy and somewhat basic. We sang traditional songs, learned a little about notation and sight-reading on a very simple, one-line level, and were told that "the greatest composers were the three B's". It is difficult to know at this distance in time just how much I actually absorbed from those once-a-week lessons, and how much was acquired from other sources. I remember the music teacher as an accomplished pianist, of fragile and pretty appearance. She was nevertheless firm and demanding.

I can never hear "Jerusalem" sung on any occasion without being aware that the precise diction and exact note-holding which she expected - and got - from all of us in this item are usually lacking, even in many professional performances; so perhaps I did learn from her at least the importance for satisfactory musical performance of discipline and technical mastery.

The lack of self-discipline and perseverance in the field of "learning music" continued. In my late teens I received the gift of a second-hand 'cello, an instrument whose sound I love, possibly above all others, and one which I dearly wanted to be able to play. I did not match dreams with determination.

During this period - it was early in the War - I attended a course of WEA classes on musical history and theory conducted by Hans Redlich, whom I got to know slightly and very much admired. He advised me that it was rather late to begin on an instrument such as the cello since my fingers were by then unlikely to have the necessary flexibility. I would be more likely to succeed if I were to study musicology rather than an instrument! I don't now remember, but strongly suspect that I may have tried to play for him, and that he was being characteristically kind and tactful. He was a very encouraging man, and from him I gained some insight into musical theory.

Apart from the radio, there were few opportunities in the locality for hearing live professional performances of classical music and travel to London once the war had started in 1939 was not often a practical proposition. Paradoxically, however, it was during the war that my own musical world burst open and I enjoyed some of my most memorable early musical experiences.

The evocation of place and occasion which music can effect is astonishingly powerful and however much one's knowledge of a work or a composer may deepen, often the basis of one's love or understanding is traceable to such first encounters. Being in ATS uniform in a wartime queue outside the Albert Hall afforded me the first chance of a cancelled ticket to hear Menuhin playing Bartok - to me at that time a totally unknown and alien composer. Menuhin's genius provided the necessary bridge between this strange music and some undiscovered receptiveness within myself, so that after forty years I can recall that performance and mark it as one of the foundations of a whole area of musical experience that has followed. Similarly, later in the war I went almost by chance to a performance in a Nottingham concert hall of Elgar's "Dream of Gerontius" in which Peter Pears was the soloist, and the overwhelmingly beautiful work became another landmark.

Does every music lover remember their first encounter with Beethoven's Ninth, I wonder? All subsequent hearings carry with them for me a kind of echo, distant yet distinct. Somewhere behind whatever performance I am currently listening to, the old '78s' are sounding through a home-designed and hand-made exponential horn. Part of me is again 19, and realising that this work is one supremely bright star, and that in the same sky are myriads of others all awaiting the discovery of the particular light they have to shed on and into our lives.

During my period at Bletchley Park, musical entertainment was always available in off-duty periods and often the concerts were of professional standard, performed by artists some of whom were to become household names after the war. Here again my musical horizons were broadened unexpectedly by contact, however slight, with trained musicians. There were also miniature transitory delights, such as on the occasion when a fellow ATS corporal with a rich, pure voice, who sang for her own pleasure whenever she could and with whom I went to several live and recorded concerts, was taking a bath in the next cubicle to mine. Suddenly the brilliant notes of the Bell Song from Lakmé soared over the sound of splashing water in that bleak, dimly-lit breeze-block barn of a bath-house, and for a few minutes those sounds were for me a more important part of activities in the camp than any code-breaking success.

There was a period of many years, when life was over-filled with a job and a family, during which it was well-nigh impossible to find any time at all when I could listen to music unhindered by mundane cares. But eventually, as the family grew up and left home there were some hours in the week when I could give a little more attention to my own personal interests and first among these has been music.

For a time I became almost obsessed, insatiable. There was so much to catch up on. Old well-loved favourite composers to return to, new, untried masters to meet. And recently, in retirement, although some chores and responsibilities must still take precedence, there are more and more hours when without a feeling of guilt it is possible to sit quietly and absorb, learn, enjoy and be made a little more whole each day by the marvellous gifts which this most universal, healing and communicative of all the arts has to bestow.

I have yet to move easily in the strange and uncompromising realm of very modern classical music, and doubt whether I shall ever now gain from it to the extent which I have from earlier works. Repeated attempts to learn some of its language are, however, bringing rewards and I shall continue to explore. But, with a few notable exceptions, my affinity and understanding seems to bring me from fairly early compositions to within a decade or so either side of my own date of birth, and I wonder if this is perhaps so with other non-practising music-lovers. Another explanation may be that significant music must inevitably reflect the era in which it is composed, and our own is perhaps the most troubled and uncertain in human history.

To me, much mid- and late-twentieth century music is harsh, threatening, uncomfortable, and its demands greater than I feel able to meet. Am I perhaps concealing behind a suspect facade a rigidity, a lack of willingness to strive for understanding? I trust not. Life should surely continue to be equated with growth in as many areas as possible until its last hold is slackened and all the faculties fail.

Interviewed during a television programme about the Tchaikovsky International Piano Competition recently, Peter Donohoe suggested that if a non-trained music lover left a concert having enjoyed it and gained something from it, no matter what opinion the professional critics might express about the performers' technical merits or faults, then that concert had been successful.

Communication to the layman, through the performer(s), of the composer's thought, inspiration or intention, was what musical performance was all about, and to me music above all is the form of communication most likely to transcend humankind's self-erected barriers. As far as its importance in my own personal development is concerned, I find I am significantly divided against myself. Increasingly catholic listening has enriched life incalculably and continues to do so.

However, into this richness is also woven a negative reaction which sometimes appears as regret or self-condemnation in that I have not pursued some form of practical music-making in order to deepen and widen my understanding and knowledge. Sometimes, the resentment that circumstances beyond my control have prevented such activity except for the most superficial tinkering, has served only to exacerbate the sense of frustration.

This particular avenue of exploration thus ends with a question; have I let circumstances dictate the course of events? If I have, would the alternative approach have been one expressing positive character traits such as courage, determination, perseverance? Or, of negative traits such as self-interest, which would have resulted in the possible neglect of others partly dependent on me, or of my job, or of any other of those activities which I have so often felt have been imposed upon me, rather than having been of my own choosing?

IV

"The Wing Wherewith we Fly"

I have many times been mistaken for a teacher by new acquaintances and I have always been quick to make a disclaimer. As with so many of my generation I was conditioned to accord to any kind of authority figure a measure of respect and I have never felt that I warrant any such deference, particularly as a result of mistaken categorisation.

(How odd most young people today would find such a notion!)

Nevertheless, education has for over 30 years been woven in and out of my life in various ways. With a husband, a son and a daughter all trained and working at one time or another as classroom teachers; having worked myself as a clerk in an Institute of Education; having typed a number of first or higher degree theses for students inside and outside the family; and having done some part-time training and employment as a youth leader and voluntarily attended courses connected with some aspect of education, I have been more than marginally interested in the subject.

For a long time I believed that a universal basic education, if administered with integrity, might be one answer to many of the world's problems. I have learned to accept that there are no short cuts to a better life for all.

A close enquiry into what is meant by education would be needed before it could be assumed that its universal application would not actually give rise to more problems than it would solve. The controversies which have raged so passionately in Britain alone in the last fifty years about most aspects of our own educational system and its implementation, ranging from such broad issues as private/state school provision, and selection procedures, to comparatively minor decisions taken by individual head teachers, are in themselves an indication of the enormously complex nature of the subject.

If one extends the consideration of education to include systems existing in other nationalities and cultures than our own, and the lack of any provision at all for vast numbers of people in many parts of the world, it is at once obvious that even if universal education could be magicked into existence overnight, the global controversies that would greet the coming of the morning would be unimaginable.

Again, it is a favourite cliché notion that everyone in the "civilized" societies of the world can consider themselves to some extent to be experts in education, since we have all been to school and can therefore in theory vouch for the effects upon us of our own experiences of education, were they good, bad., or totally irrelevant. Like many clichés, there is a tiny basis of truth in such a claim, but the paradox is that if the particular education experienced was either bad or irrelevant, the result will presumably have been to fail to equip one to make an objective and considered judgment as to the quality of that education.

The immense responsibility assumed by anyone who decides to become a school teacher - in whatever category - bears comparison only with that of becoming a parent. No other occupation affects so totally the lives of every citizen (excepting of course only those so impaired as to be uneducable). Thus, what motivates an aspiring teacher is of prime importance, and unfortunately there are many - certainly in this country and presumably everywhere else - whose reasons for joining the education industry are somewhat suspect. Nothing less than an honest commitment to the ideal of giving others some of the means of becoming greater versions of themselves seems to me to be sufficient. Only with such an aim, surely, can a teacher be other than an arrogant seeker of power over the lives of others.

As to the content of what is taught, that is not part of my self-appointed brief here, even could it be contained in anything less than a whole library of books. If the reason for the teaching - either choice of content or method - is an honest belief in the value of knowledge for its own sake and for the total enrichment of the learner, then surely the result must be a positive gain for each individual involved and thus ultimately for humankind in general.

So, what have I done, and what am I doing, to further this particular interest, and where has it led me in this more immediate search? There are perhaps three aspects to an answer.

Firstly, I have supposedly nurtured others so as to support their more direct involvement in the process of education.

Secondly, I have tried - though often not dedicatedly enough - to learn what I could along the way, to help me to understand, appreciate and contribute towards the efforts of others in their work.

Thirdly, in small, unconnected and spasmodic episodes, I have perhaps been a tiny version of an educator myself. Obviously one teaches one's own children to some degree, both consciously and by accident. More formally and deliberately, a decision to try part-time youth work in the 1960's had in it an element of a wish to show a few young people some of the ways in which they might choose to grow in awareness of themselves. Latterly, I have been trying to help just one young person to achieve greater literacy, so continuing this particular thread in the fabric.

A period around 1949-50 as a clerk at the University of Leeds Institute of Education provided opportunity for daily contact with several individuals concerned with the administration of higher education. The informal discussions, which often arose from these contacts, suggested to me that had I earlier acquired the necessary paper qualifications I might perhaps have been sitting on the other side of the table....

Too late, however - another "if only..." In 1951, our first child was born, and raising a family then took priority over any other activity. I do not for a moment imagine that the cause of education was in fact set back by any noticeable amount!

In the 1960's, having moved from Leeds to Derbyshire, and with the family growing more independent and a part-time clerical job in a local geriatric hospital which didn't seem to overstretch my capabilities, I took on evening work with young people in both formal and informal settings. The sessions were centered mostly on "drama" and if the "customers" learned as much as I did from our activities, these must be accounted at least partially successful. Some of the liveliest periods started when up to a dozen 14 - 16 year olds, all male, who had not signed up for any of one club's more traditional activities, were put on to my register and told by the club leader that they were going to "do drama" with me.

They were initially antagonistic, on the whole physically big, very noisy, and more than ready to "take the mickey". I was unprepared, untrained and conditioned to a very conventional view of what drama groups should achieve.

To this day, I cannot be sure what came to my rescue, it could have been any one of many factors. Perhaps along the way I had picked up more than I realised of educational theory and practice. Perhaps the challenge of coping for the first time ever with a group of lively, working-class adolescent lads put me on my mettle; perhaps they just decided that they liked me. Whatever the reason, within half-an-hour they were co-operating in an imaginative improvisation on the theme of a mountain rescue, and enjoying it hugely, if noisily. I did wonder about liability for injury, or damage to Education Committee property when they piled up chairs and desks to suggest the mountain before I could intervene.

Luckily no one fell, nothing was broken, and thereafter the group flourished for many months. Those lads must now be in their thirties; - do any of them, I wonder, ever think back to the fun we had together in those rather dingy classrooms, and did it help them to learn anything about themselves and life, as it did me?

They showed me how far a group will let a bully, or a show-off, work out his aggressions before they decide that he is spoiling their enjoyment or their learning. They gave me a partial insight into the shock they suffered when they moved from a nine-to-four school day on their last Friday as pupils, to the following Monday's eight-to-six hard graft on a factory bench or a shift down the pit. They demonstrated in many an evening's improvised sketches, or discussions of one-act play scripts, the vulnerability concealed beneath their brash and cocky exteriors.

An outing to the local repertory production was for many of them the first time they had ever been inside a theatre, and their shrewd if unsophisticated observations afterwards gave me a refreshingly new view of the contribution which drama might - but mostly didn't at that time - make to the average person's life.

Referring back to what I wrote nearly eight years ago about learning to ask questions, it now seems that that idea needs to be expanded to embrace not only the asking of questions, but the interaction of ideas, thoughts, experiences. Our education should above all alert us to the potentialities, not only within ourselves, but within others too. It should offer as many opportunities as possible for appreciating the singular importance of our own and every other creature's place in the environment, and the contribution each can make towards understanding ourselves and others more completely.

V

<u>"A Thousand Several Tongues"</u>

In the drawing-room, dimly lit by gas-mantles on either side of the fireplace, we (my father, mother, brother and myself) sat amid yards and yards of pale blue and yellow petersham ribbon - the sort that was extensively used at the time (the 1920's) for trimmings on women's hats.

We were making rosettes which would be used in a coming election campaign. I have no earlier memory of anything connected with politics. I assume that my father, who was at one time a Liberal, was either standing for local council elections or was working in support of the party for a pending General Election. He was in the hat trade, which no doubt explained the vast quantities of ribbon.

By the time I developed even the flimsiest form of political awareness, he had joined the Conservative Party, the Rotarians, and was a Freemason. I do not remember ever having a serious political discussion with him, or indeed with anyone else, until some time after I had left home. My mother, who publicly supported his activities throughout their lives, once said to me that she remained a Liberal inwardly, but how she voted I never knew.

Politics, therefore, was not an issue in my life as a very young person. I didn't think things through, although I was gradually made aware that there were many, many contradictions in the sort of life styles I encountered.

Possibly the earliest stirrings of anything even resembling a social conscience occurred when I was asked to help at a Chapel Jumble Sale for the first time. I suppose I was twelve or thirteen. When the doors opened and the first surge of customers fought their way to the trestle tables piled high with cast-off garments - some of my own doubtless among them - I was astonished. The desperation that could motivate human beings to claw their way forward to secure a grubby second-hand dress for two pence, shoes for three, was something I hadn't known existed. I was in a state of shock for most of the evening, and when it was all over, I went home and cried.

I did nothing more about it however, and my apathy and blindness shame me now. Oh yes, we used to help with flag days, and missionary collections, and concerts for orphanage funds, and all the other self-righteous activities which made us feel that we were guiltless of neglecting our "less fortunate brethren". But as for considering ways of actually changing things, however infinitesimally, so that life would be more socially just for a few more of our fellow human beings, most of the people I knew behaved as though living righteously, attending Chapel (or Church), praying, and giving to charity were sufficient.

And I, cocooned, moderately privileged, trying to be good and to emulate my betters, conformed. Among friends at school in my mid-teens, however, there was one who took a close interest in the Spanish Civil War, and whose boyfriend joined the International Brigade. My own reaction on hearing of this bore a marked relationship to the Peter Pan syndrome - "to die would be an awfully big adventure" - rather than eliciting an examination of the principles involved.

My response to the arrival of our evacuees in the early part of the war was similarly incurious. Robert and Peggy (I have forgotten their real names) were from London's East End and were a living indictment of social conditions in that part of the capital in 1940, wartime conditions notwithstanding. They were under-nourished, dirty, and had lice-infected heads, but they both had attractive personalities. Mother duly de-nitted them and bathed them, and made or bought them warm clothing to replace their pitifully inadequate wardrobes. Robert - I think he was about eight years old - made scarcely any protest about anything. Indeed I now realise that he was either somewhat retarded, or was in a state of shock as a result of the upheaval that war had brought into his life. He was certainly eneuretic (wet the bed) throughout his stay with us. Peggy, who was five, loudly screamed her objections to all attempts to clean her up, but in the end emerged from her first-ever bath pale, thin and sweet-smelling.

Neither of them knew what a toothbrush was. Peggy, on being shown where she would sleep, gently stroked the bed covers, looked up at us from huge, dark-ringed eyes and said very quietly, "Is this really for me?" It appeared that at home she had no bed, but slept under the kitchen table.

They didn't stay with us for very long and were fetched back to London by, I think, their mother, although my memory here is very hazy. What I am sure of is that, despite sharing my parents' compassion for Robert and Peggy, and trying to help a little with the day-to-day caring for them, at no time did I look deeply into the implications of their obvious deprivation - material, educational or social; - and I was by then in my late teens,

Earlier, such events as the General Strike of 1926, the Jarrow Marches, blind ex-soldiers from the First World War selling matches, the Mosley rallies - all had seemed to happen somewhere outside my world, leaving my real self untouched. The nature of our formal education certainly made no overt contribution to political awareness. I remember no attempts to link the content of the history syllabus, for example, with the current state of society either in the UK or elsewhere. Sympathy for those whom we would today describe as deprived was certainly encouraged, but analysis of cause and effect, social or economic theories, were never offered.

My brother had a subject on his timetable called "Civics" so presumably boys were given some information about the organisation of society; possibly such matters were not considered suitable for girls.

There were occasional references to social ills in discussions at the Chapel of course, but these were naturally circumscribed by religious conventions. Indeed, convention - religious and social - governed thought and action in most areas of life among my immediate friends and family. In the late 1930's for instance, Moral Rearmament was a growing movement, but it was regarded with suspicion by more than one sector of society. I did join the Peace Pledge Union, since pacifism seemed to be morally right, but this was a gut reaction rather than the result of informed political reasoning.

When the war began in 1939, that plank of pacifism was knocked from beneath me and initially I was bewildered and uncertain about where I stood. It soon became apparent that the most important and immediate task was to defeat Fascism; - afterwards there would be time to consider how we wanted to see our society develop. But I still had no clear idea about the causes of the rise of Fascism in Europe. I only knew that the Nazi rallies, the Russian purges, the American treatment of black people - all these and much else seemed equally abhorrent. However, if Nazi domination were successful it would mean the end of our society as we knew it, which still had many freedoms despite its shortcomings. Even the vaguest dreams about planning a more just social order would be useless unless we defeated the enemy outside.

The course of the war years as I lived them is detailed in another part of this record, but obviously natural maturation, together with the influences of the many people, institutions and ideas I encountered between 1939 and 1945, served to change considerably my thinking and my beliefs. Although once again my lack of mental alertness and vigour resulted in only a superficial recognition of cause and effect. I still lived largely by ill-defined feelings about what was good and desirable rather than by convictions based on reasoning.

One of the first casualties of this period in my development was the loss of faith in conventional religion. Neither the tenets from an early Methodist upbringing nor those from a later brief acquaintance with the Anglican Church seemed to offer foolproof answers to the searching questions posed by the war and by the contradictions abounding in British society.

I was thrown back onto a naive and less than satisfactory idea that there seemed to be evidence for the existence of opposing abstract forces for good and evil which profoundly affect all human existence. Beyond that, or how to relate it to everyday life, I could not see.

Another area where rigid principles were jettisoned was that of sexual morality. The moral judgments I had absorbed from childhood died hard, but I began to accept the possibility that not only were there many forms of love but also that there are many sins more dangerous and deadly than, say, sexual infidelity or "illegitimate" motherhood. Personal relationships obviously played a part in these changed attitudes but a growing recognition of the facts of political and social immorality also had its place.

Not, however, until my own children began to grow up, ask questions, formulate ideas, reject ready-made philosophies and challenge some of my views, did I actively adopt some kind of thought-out political stance. I am still exploring the extent of that stance, and still adjusting almost daily to its implications. I have again, as in the late 1930's, embraced pacifism although now it is from studied conviction rather than instinct.

I become more and more sceptical of the worth of the contribution which organised party politics (at least in this country) can or do make to the betterment of life for the individual, who seems to matter less and less to the professional policy makers. Being a gradualist, I shrink from the idea of violent revolution but there are many occasions in the present apparent increase in political polarisation of interests when that seems to me the inevitable route to the ultimate goal of social justice.

The wicked cynicism which appears to be inseparable from all forms of material power, be that power political, industrial, economic or deriving from individual wealth/privilege, needs to be exposed and opposed at every level.

The question of how best that fight can be pursued will probably be answered differently by each person of whom it is asked. From improved education to religious conversion, from revolution to increased alleviation of poverty, from benevolent dictatorship to the destruction of multi-national corporations - theories are not in short supply.

What does seem to me to be signally lacking in the collective body is simple compassion, human caring, respect for life - in fact a vision of all life as being a potential expression of dignity and love from birth to death. If enough people had access to the inner power of such a vision of life, the obscenities of starvation, armaments, exploitation, racism, drug trafficking and many others might become extinct.

Preaching a gospel - any gospel - I believe to be suspect.

Propaganda usually contains at least some element of untruth. Imposed solutions will always be resisted to greater or lesser degree. What is left as a means of harnessing the strength inherent in the idea of how they want life to be, which I am certain is held by the majority of the world's materially powerless millions?

Perhaps genuine communication is one outstandingly important factor. Here I feel that I am beginning to reach one of the outer limits of the territory I began to explore when I started this whole enterprise.

Woolly pieties, naive theories, moralising just will not serve and my intellectual capacities appear to be inadequate to take me much further. By considering a few random examples of what I see as genuine communication, I may arrive at a clearer view. I see it as occurring, for instance:

when parents and teachers genuinely listen to children's questions and try to give honest answers;

when creative artists (gardeners, architects, even fashion designers, as well as poets, painters and musicians) use their media in attempts to serve, and. to widen humanity's view of itself, rather than for self- indulgent or commercial reasons;

when voluntary and paid workers in charities and other caring organisations involve themselves in their work as co-operators with their "clients" and not as benefactors, easing their own consciences;

when supporters of causes are able to express that support solely in terms of a willingness to share their ideas and strengths (as in the Greenham Common Peace Camp), rather than by attempts to use a cause for their personal aggrandisement;

where there is supportive interaction between patients and carers, say, in hospital wards where all too frequently an atmosphere of insensitivity is characteristic.

The relevance of some of the foregoing ideas to my attempt to formulate a personal political creed lies in the proposition that apart from some of our most personal relationships, almost all areas of our lives have a political element.

The development of the women's movement in recent years has drawn attention to the extent to which political factors affect us, men and women alike, in ways previously considered to be quite personal, domestic, a-political. Stripped of much that is, I suggest, bizarre, exhibitionist, self-indulgent and blatantly commercial, the movement is still left with a very considerable contribution to offer as an example of an agency uniquely suited to assist communication between individuals, groups, organisations, parties, races, nations.

What, however, of "negative communication"? There is a kind of communication, distorted though it may be, between a torturer and his victim; a pet-owner and his ill-treated animal; farmers hoarding their grain in anticipation of increased profits and the starving in poor countries; arms dealers and the losers in a war. Simply to let other people know how little regard you have for them as fellow creatures does not in any way help them in their search for purpose or happiness in their lives.

The more all men and women can be enabled to recognise each other as formed from the same inherent matter, yet with an infinite number of variations in the disposition of that matter, the better surely will humankind be enabled to discover some kind of increased harmony. If more of us try to analyse the causes underlying negative communication as well as to acknowledge the urgent need for positive interchange, we may be able to add a tidy sum to the desperately meagre amount of mutual understanding so far deposited in our planet's joint spiritual bank account.

VI

"Affections of Delight"

There are those who seem to find little difficulty in setting down the intimacies of their emotional development for others to read. I am not among their number. To examine the history of any of the significant relationships in my life will be the hardest task of all for me and I have left it nearly to the last. It was on my original route-map, but when I came to consider the implications of that section I decided to by-pass it.

Now I acknowledge that that would be the coward's way, and I want very much to have the courage to face myself with as much of the whole truth as possible, and if communication (even with oneself) is so essential a part of life as I insist, what is a life-story without an account of its significant relationships?

Of the most important earliest of these, I have already given some indication. My Mother once said to me, after I was quite adult, that she felt she had failed me as a mother. I found this an amazing misconception and tried hard and often afterwards to demonstrate to her how much I valued what she had done for and meant to me. I still have her last letter, written when she was quite ill, to comfort me with the knowledge that I did eventually succeed in assuring her that she had been quite mistaken so to regard herself. But I now know, as a parent of grown-up children myself, what she was experiencing when she made that remark.

We want so much for our offspring, and try as we might to afford them eventually a life as mentally and materially independent as possible of our own ambitions and desires for them, it requires a very deep wisdom indeed to maintain the right balance of disinterested cherishing.

My father's love for my brother and myself expressed itself in ways which I found more difficult to identify with, the older I grew. When I was still small it was easy to enjoy his company. His games with us were gentle, he was always concerned about our development and achievements, and on outings and holidays we did interesting and enjoyable things all together. As the years passed though, the number of ways in which our viewpoints differed began to increase and to raise barriers, and eventually there were few subjects we could discuss significantly without the threat of tension. He was ambitious for us both, but his goals were not mine, nor, I think, my brother's.

In retrospect I see my father as a frustrated man who had in many senses lost his way. His dogmatic, brook-no-contradiction views on most subjects probably revealed that he had never managed to break through his own particular barrier of received opinions and of an apparently uncritical acceptance of what it suited him to believe. But since we rarely found it easy as adults to enjoy interchange at a deep level, I cannot be sure that I am right. The gateway through which I saw him pass into old age and increasing dependence was opened on the day when, for the first time ever, he sought my opinion and advice about some practical matters connected with his and Mother' decision to give up their own home and go into a Masonic Home for the Elderly.

I hope his last years were as serene as they seemed to be, and that his repeated protestations about how comfortable and happy they both were there did not indicate a deep resentment at not being in full and independent control of his life to the end.

Of all the other relatives who were part of my growing up,

two or three stand out with especial clarity.

My paternal grandmother was the only member of that generation of my family surviving when I was born, and she died when I was about twelve. She was sweet-faced, short and plump, and her knuckles were swollen with arthritic lumps which, child-like, I once compared to door-knobs, and from then on she shared this observation with me as a joke. Such swellings are no joke, Grandma, as I can now testify from my own experience! I never saw her wearing any garment other than long black dresses with high stiffened collars, and fastened with countless jet buttons, and for most of the time she wore over them a large white starched apron which she called her flag.

Two of her children, both unmarried, lived with her and stayed on in the family house after she died. My Aunt K----, the youngest in the family, was an infant school teacher and Uncle S---- worked in the hat trade.

But without doubt the most colourful character in the whole of our family album was my father's eldest sister R----. In my early childhood she lived in east London with her giant of a husband and their only son, and we saw them rarely. On being widowed she moved back to live next door to her old home in our town. All the family had tried for years to stem her flow of words but none of their strategies had ever worked.

Never have I met such a talker! She would frequently say "Stop me if I've told you this before..." and even as my father was already answering, "Yes, you have R----, give it a rest," she was away with whatever anecdote it was, and nothing could stay her. I remember one family meal when, in full verbal spate, she picked up the wrong shaker and had liberally dusted her apple-pie with pepper instead of sugar before any of us could get a word in to warn her.

Aunt R---- was also a great needlewoman, and one Christmas she sent me a beautiful party frock, hand-made from layer upon layer of soft georgette, graded from pale orange at the waist to scarlet at the hem. I wept with disappointment when I tried to put it on and found that she had made it to my last year's measurements.

She was also, in her own estimation, an experienced counsellor in matters of the heart, and encouraged me to consult her on every occasion when such concerns were affecting me as I grew into adolescence. In fact, what she really loved doing best was talking about her own life and loves, and in particular describing over and over again her wedding day when, she claimed, the Chapel (a several hundred-seater building) had been so full that extra chairs had had to be placed in the aisles!

In her failing, solitary last years, poor Aunt R---- grew increasingly strange. The wigs she had been wont to wear to conceal her premature baldness were replaced with an assortment of misshapen tea cosies, and a foul-smelling oil heater became her only means of cooking and warmth. I dreaded the moments on my visits when she produced a less than clean mug full of paraffin-flavoured tea. But, odd, unhygienic, lonely as she was, to the end she kept up the floods of talk which no-one could dam. If there is an after-life, as she believed, I wonder how they cope there with voluble eccentrics?

Of my Mother's siblings I met only two - her sister L---- and her youngest brother F----, who is still alive and with whom I have kept in contact by letter since Mother died, though I scarcely knew him at all before then.

Mother remained closely attached to my Aunt L----
throughout her life, and I spent many happy times with
Aunty and her husband F---- in Peckham. They enjoyed
house-moving and had changed council houses and flats
thirteen times in their married life, always in the South East
area of London which they loved. Uncle had started his
working life as a post-office messenger boy, and they married
before the first world war on his wages of around £1 per
week. They would tell me how they used to enjoy a night out
in Peckham, to include "the pictures", fish and chips and a
drink, for about 1/- (1 shilling = 5p).

The council house they occupied for most of the period when I
was young backed onto a railway line, and under a bridge just
round the corner my brother and I used to stand to hear the
"thunder" as the electric trains - a great novelty to us who
knew only steam engines at home - went rattling over our
heads.

I loved these holidays - walks in a London park; the fair on
Peckham Rye; visits to the picture house where they still had
"turns" between the films and, a cinema organ that rose,
flooded in coloured lights, from under the floor. Waiting up
until ten o'clock to greet Uncle when he returned from his
evening delivery round; the fat albums of colourful romantic
picture postcards which he had sent home from the trenches.
He was in France through most of the 14-18 war and returned
home whole to tell his tales. The cabinet full to bursting with
souvenirs, many in miniature Goss china, of their daytrips to
the seaside - all these scenes are vivid in my mind.

I suppose this was because I was encountering at close
quarters a life-style quite different from that of my own home
and was at the same time in the company of two warm people
who, with few material luxuries, I never once heard complain.
They even managed to spare something now and then to help

the family next door - a sickly mother, a father not at work and two young children who were, I suspect, often hungry. If my Aunt and Uncle habitually had margarine instead of butter and were not too proud to accept the occasional tactful offer of help from my Mother, what sort of shortages did that family next-door experience?

A long-forgotten incident suddenly comes to mind. It was from R----, the son of that family, that I received my first-ever love letter. We were both about nine or ten at the time. He was a black-haired, olive-skinned boy, handsome in the romantic way which sometimes accompanies ill-health. His large dark eyes were fringed with very long lashes, and there was a mini-drama one day when he took my aunt's scissors and tried to cut the lashes short after having been teased about such a feature being girlish. This action was somehow tied up with his written declaration of love, but the details are vague.

It is a truism that for most of us growing up in the 1930's in my sort of environment, ideas about relationships between women and men were firmly based on romance and strongly influenced by the cinema and popular fiction. There were occasional odd, difficult-to-reconcile hints of relationships that did not fit into the predictable pattern of girl sooner or later meeting Mr. Right, being wooed, won and settling down to domestic bliss.

There were sometimes hushed, not-in-front-of-the-children references to scandalous goings-on at boys' schools, a divorce in some respectable local family might be the subject of shocked whispers. There was one girl in our peer group who had an illegitimate baby, and another who, at 17, married a widower nearly twice her age and became a mother while most of us were still at school. On the whole, we expected that life would present us with the kind of personal situations which we saw as normal, apparently working satisfactorily, and leading from first kiss to eventual grandparenthood.

But of course there were in those uneasy years before 1939 many other currents in other areas of society and now, whenever I see television programmes or read books about some of the excesses and aberrations, the philosophies and life-styles which existed - though we never then became aware of them - I find them deeply disturbing, more so than many of the horrors in other periods of history. I can only conclude that this is because they suggest that I and my kind were living a life so totally unreal that we must all have been dream-people, our relationships as insubstantial as wraiths.

At the time, however, we saw ourselves as very much alive and of this world as we set off in our cycling groups to see the latest Astaire/Rodgers extravaganza, or put on our long frocks and daringly bright make-up to go dancing until midnight, and then walk five miles home.

I wish I knew my brother better. Six years is an awkward gap in age between siblings of different sex and at the one time when we might have drawn closer in our late teens, wartime separations prevented this. I suspect that we have more than our parentage in common, but somehow we have never discovered each other.

The effect of the outbreak of war on my most personal relationships was considerable. In 1939 I was already engaged to be married to a trainee Methodist minister, who hoped to become a missionary. I had accepted his proposal in the honest belief that the sort of life we would lead together was utterly right for me. There had been other boyfriends before him, one of whom - several years older than myself - had seemed at one time to be my Mr. Right. However, I had felt unable to match his expectations of a rich intellectual companionship and the relationship faltered and finally ended when I heard indirectly about an important decision he had taken about his future of which he had given me no inkling and in which I was therefore presumably not included.

With the changes in contacts, demands, opportunities and beliefs occasioned by the war, I realised that life as a minister's wife would be total hypocrisy for me and I broke my engagement to the potential missionary.

I met D. in the early months of the war, and knew immediately that whatever our respective futures might hold there was the sort of affinity between us which was something very rare and that no matter what happened to each of us that special bond would always survive. The war parted us many times, and in many ways. I made more than one close relationship in those years, and even got engaged again, only to break it off when I acknowledged that a lifetime with the man in question would be a travesty of what I believed marriage could be. Happily, when D. and I met again towards the end of the war, it took us only a few hours to confirm the survival of our earlier empathy, and within six weeks, we were married.

There are no universally applicable rules for a good marriage. Each partnership has to work out its own strategies for survival and, any man or woman who claims that a long joint life has been totally "happy" or easy is either a fool or a self-deceiver. But if the joys, the sharing, the mutual discoveries, the giving and accepting of support are worth anything at all to each party, they are worth striving to preserve when the going gets rough - as undoubtedly it sometimes must when two individuals have elected to become a pair.

The romantic notions of gratuitous conjugal bliss are still being pedalled today - albeit in more subtle and subliminal ways - just as they were in the thirties by Hollywood and by women's magazines. I believe they are as much to blame for the failure of many relationships as is that school of thought which tries to teach that total freedom can of itself bring happiness. To achieve any real rewards communication in every meaning of the word between a man and a woman must be as total and as deep as we can make it, even if that sometimes hurts.

That childbirth is at once so everyday and so miraculous an event is possibly the most supreme paradox in the human experience. From the earliest stage of my first pregnancy I looked forward with confidence to becoming a mother. I subscribed with enthusiasm to Grantley Dick Read's theories on "natural childbirth" and earnestly practised relaxation procedures. I should have known better than to accept uncritically the advice of a man in the matter of how to perform the one act that men can't achieve!

Nowhere in Dr. Dick Read's teachings do I remember reading any advice about how to cope, either physically or psychologically, if something even slightly abnormal occurred. True, I had a "good" pregnancy, ailments and discomforts were minimal, and I was able to keep active throughout, even including an energetic day's visit to the Festival of Britain not long before the confinement.

In the event however, due to complications which arose during labour, the birth was almost as far removed from "natural" as it could have been. I had agreed to be a "guinea-pig" for a midwifery training school towards the end of pregnancy, and one student midwife was the only person who hinted that there might be some difficulty and her theory was dismissed by everyone else concerned.

My son was delivered by forceps whilst I was under total anaesthetic and for his first few days of life he was in special care and I did not see him. I have always been, and still remain, convinced that the lack of bonding between us in those early hours of his existence, however desirable it was thought to be in the light of the medical knowledge of the day, was at least partly responsible for the fact that it took us perhaps twenty years or more to establish a satisfactory mother/son relationship. Even so, had I not had that hospital confinement we might not today even have a son, so I try to keep these thoughts in perspective.

In the 1950's most second and subsequent children were born at home and so it was with our daughter and because it was a normal birth in familiar surroundings, I am sure that my whole attitude to her nurturing was different.

The close attachments enjoyed within my immediate family have been and are, without doubt, the source not only of my greatest joys but also of much of my inner growth. Despite periods of tension and misunderstanding which are a normal part of every united family's development, our continued and deepening caring for each other has led to the kind of stability which has made it possible for me to write this book, primarily for them.

Somewhere in all these memories, there should be a place for recollections of animal acquaintances and friends. Of the very first one, I have only reported evidence. My Mother never appeared to be fond of dogs and this may be attributable to the fact that when I was an infant, the family pet dog, a Pomeranian who used to guard my cradle while I slept, once made the mistake of taking up his station not at the foot of the cot but at its head and she found him lying across my face. Fortunately, I survived none the worse, but the "Pom" did not.

Next, I remember a cat who chose to have her kittens in our kitchen. I was sent from the room on that occasion; very disappointed to miss what I was sure would have been a most enlightening spectacle.

One year I was given a canary as a birthday present and it was understood that I should be totally responsible for its care. So solemnly did I accept this charge, that I jealously refused to let my brother talk to it, or to help me clean the cage, or replenish the food and drinking containers. It was "my" bird, and he wasn't even to encourage it to sing for him!

Later, my father kept a greyhound which he sometimes raced. It seemed an unlovable sort of dog to me and quite lost any little charm it might have had when one day, as I bent down to fondle its head, it turned to look up at me and one of its strong teeth knocked a piece off one of my own.

There were no more domestic pets in my parents' household after this, and other encounters with dogs were equally unfortunate. I was once bitten quite badly on my bottom by a passing Airedale terrier, outside our home, and forced into the indignity of sitting in a bowl of warm disinfectant water in the kitchen while the family looked on anxiously as the water turned red from my bleeding bite.

In the early days of our marriage, we took in a stray kitten. This poor creature didn't last long - it became home to a vicious infestation of fleas and had to be destroyed.

When our own children were small, we acquired another cat who became part of the family for several years. He wasn't a very intelligent animal and uncharacteristically for a cat seemed to court disaster by his clumsiness. Even so, when he developed a severe skin complaint and had to be taken away by the vet for the sake of our children's health, we all missed him sorely.

Of all the relationships I have personally witnessed between human beings and animals, that of our last dog with ourselves was the most remarkable. She was a Sheltie, given to our daughter as a 16th birthday present, and when A. left home to go to College, Tammy came to belong virtually to D. and myself.

I had initially been firmly against the introduction of any more pets, particularly a dog, into our home. I was quite well aware that the day-to-day care and responsibility would ultimately be mine, whatever the good intentions and protestations of everyone else. I was overruled, and Tammy came, staying in the family for 11½ years.

The empathy between all of us developed into something very special. Only other pet-owners who have experienced this level of closeness ever truly understand it, and it is something which has much to teach us about ourselves if only we wish to learn.

As soon as an animal is taken into a home, that creature is placed in a state of total dependency upon the human being(s) concerned. Unlike a human being, however, it will never grow to achieve self-reliance, never be able to feed itself or cure its ailments. This vulnerability is an attribute which can draw out both the best and the worst of human characteristics. (I freely acknowledge that I came to recognise in my own response to this particular obligation both an impatience and an unselfishness which I had not known I was capable of.) And through it all the animal's unquestioning devotion and companionship so totally without guile leads to a relationship subtly different than any between human and human, and brings an added dimension to our experience.

And when at the last one has to acknowledge that the time has come for the little share of life held in that creature's frame to be given up; when it is abundantly obvious that the pain and discomfort can no longer be supported, ah! then how very deep down one has to search to find the true selflessness which can make such a decision on another living being's behalf, and abide by it.

For whatever reason - and there are many, most of them selfish, - I do not expect to have any more pets.

VII

<u>"Do Thy Worst, old Time"</u>

Metaphors of archaeology and travel have been convenient hooks on which to hang some of the ideas explored so far. Now, however, in trying to reach some conclusions about the success or failure of my efforts, they no longer suffice.

I imagine that I have, in fact, been experiencing what popular psychology would call an identity crisis - and a fairly prolonged one at that! - and am at last emerging on the other side.

Self-analysis is a notoriously hazardous undertaking and I feel a moderate sense of triumph that, however faulty and incomplete my effort's have been to accomplish even part of such a task, they have in the end convinced me that there <u>has</u> been a sort of consistency in my life - a fact which I had hitherto doubted. I also believe that I shall be less reluctant in future to refer to myself rather than to others in order to assess the wisdom of any course of action I may be contemplating.

Nonetheless, on re-reading these pages I am not very proud of the image of myself that has emerged. It shows many characteristics I would rather were not there, self-satisfaction, a tendency to middle-class insensitivity, patronisation, dilettantism, and indecisiveness.

Even so, the attempt to discipline myself to try to reach some sort of answers to questions, which have hovered on the fringe of consciousness for so long, has not been a total waste of time; some answers have emerged.

Writing about oneself can be construed as a monstrously egocentric pastime, particularly if one's life hasn't been, in the accepted sense of the term, at all remarkable. Perhaps few people outside my family will ever read this, as I suggested on the first page. That doesn't detract from the benefit I have derived from "thinking on paper" - the best way I know to sort out my thoughts. And so, hopefully, I am now more completely ME than when I started, and if I believe in ME at all, I must perforce have just that little more to give out than I had before.

It is now time to explore a few last ideas for trying to keep what has been called a "contract with life".

The changed day to day routines of life at 60+ have made it possible to take note of some other spheres of interest which offer an almost limitless field for expansion of activities, exploration and self-realisation, dependent only upon physical and mental good health. This last proviso indeed is in itself a subject for further thought and investigation.

As a result of working in a geriatric hospital and of having fairly close contact with ageing relatives and friends, it has become increasingly obvious to me that the experience of growing old in Britain at the present time is a matter demanding ever more public and personal attention. Recently some books, together with the press, radio and television have indicated a growing concern with the implications of a situation where ageing is almost always defined as a problem.

This is but one example of the dangers courted by a complicated and highly-organised society which rushes to categorise people into groups and then to investigate the potential problem they pose. Babies, children, teenagers, women, men, the elderly - all are first and foremost individual human beings. Perhaps if those around them, and those who claim or aspire to cater for their needs, regarded them primarily as personalities with requirements arising from their individuality rather than from their age-groups, their race, their socio-economic class or whatever, some of the difficulties in making provision for their particular needs would disappear. This seems to be particularly true in the case of the ageing.

Although there are a few - desperately too few - caring, experienced and well-qualified experts helping to educate opinion in this field, in general attitudes to old people tend to be patronising, or uninformedly sentimental, or downright dismissive. There is certainly no easy answer, no one solution, to the practical difficulties of helping all individuals to retain their dignity, their interest in life, their continuing development as persons, once the ageing process begins to take a serious toll of mental and physical capabilities and independence.

Nevertheless, to sweep all those over 65 into the "geriatric" category for the purposes of Health and Social Service administration procedures (which then inevitably conditions the perception and appreciation of the rest of society) seems arrogant and insulting.

Many people over 65 to whom I have talked do not give priority, in their consideration of their self-image, to their chronological age. But other people's attitudes to them often force them to pay increasing attention to that particular factor, to the detriment of other aspects of their lives. To emphasise that one is "wonderful for your age" inevitably causes some people to wonder whether they are behaving unsuitably in the framework of the stereotype fashioned for them by society. Others get a false sense of pride when they hear the phrase, and imagine that simply to have reached, say, 75 and still to be able, for instance, to hold a sensible conversation, is of itself noteworthy.

It would be good to think that you are, in fact, simply you - warts (arthritis, bladder problems) and all - at 80+, just as you were you at 8, 18, 28 and. all the other stages in your life.

Further consideration of the current tendency to categorise people might be profitable. The word "teenager" tends often to be synonymous with hooligan or trouble maker; "housewife" with boredom/stagnation; and "elderly" as I have indicated, with problem. Facile labelling is liable to destroy the totality of individual personalities and there is surely benefit to be derived from a practical attempt on all our parts to respond to this emphasis on a single aspect of our selves by stressing that one aspect is only part of a whole.

A "single parent" may indeed be caring alone for a two-year-old, but there are surely many other attributes in that person's existence. A "pensioner" may no longer work, but there are more facets to life than wage-earning. The label too often masks the richness and variety of the content.

I have the impression that when I was a child, individuals - apart from categorisation by class - were seen much more as personalities, each with their own contribution to make to the social environment, labelling being restricted rather to personal names and characters than to groupings, with their consequent expectations of "typical" behaviours.

Now, although the class basis may have changed somewhat in emphasis and expression it remains as strong a labeller as ever, but to its divisive effects have been added many others as a result of society's tendency to adopt group-based. expectations - economic, racial, chronological and many more.

So one objective I set myself is to try to regard and to respond to other people totally as selves, as I regard my own self - full of individual quirks and needs, often inconsistent, contradictory, but real and not a stereotype.

The increased personal freedom I now enjoy requires in itself considerable attention. There is much temptation to wallow in the realisation that one can in fact sit and do almost nothing for a good deal of the time, and after so many years of pressured time tabling and the squeezing in of vital tasks, such temptation is sometimes hard to resist. That there is a place for sheer idling occasionally is important to recognise; but the adjustment to the notion that an hours light reading is a legitimate and even a beneficial use of time is hard to make.

Far more satisfying and rewarding is the realisation at the end of a day that one has done something new, taken up an unfamiliar activity, worked really hard at some task simply because it appealed to you and no-one else had required you to do it. So far, after nearly two years, the novelty of this situation still predominates. I do not want to waste any single hour of however many days, months, years may lie ahead before I become incapable of making such choices.

Among all the options available to me, it seems fairly certain that music, writing and further education (and this last is capable of the widest possible interpretation) will continue to fill a fair proportion of the time. The variety of subjects offered, for example, by local authority and WEA classes provides a stimulus to gain new knowledge, even if one finds some subjects to be of only passing interest.

Incidentally, the fact that attendees at such classes are often predominantly middle-aged to elderly women probably indicates how much women feel they have missed out in a number of ways, for much the same reasons as prompted me to start writing this record.

A childhood spent on the edge of the Chiltern hills gave me

many opportunities for being in close contact with the natural world. Within a few minutes' walk of the house we could climb the gentle chalk slopes, and. enjoy the sight and scent of the flowers - harebells, wild thyme, mignonette, scabious, "piggy's trotters" and many others, all with their attendant insect life. There were streams where we caught tadpoles and sticklebacks and could watch frogs about their business, and the trees and fields which were home for the birds.

A little further afield, taken by the grown-ups, we explored beech woods, commons, watercress brooks, and other country delights. We were lucky enough to enjoy a holiday at the sea each year, and - more by chance than intent - we absorbed the different nature of the wildlife offered by the beaches and the sea's edge.

After childhood a fair proportion of my life was lived in cities or towns, but an interest in natural history re-stimulated by the outstanding contributions offered in this sphere by television programmes (one of the few totally worthwhile achievements of that medium) is now claiming some of my attention. I recognise that a deeper and better understanding of all life on earth, not only that of human beings, may be illuminating in an attempt to appreciate our own role as well as being a fascinating study in its own right.

A sincere commitment to the work (and even more significantly to the philosophy) of Oxfam ensures that there need never be a day in which I could honestly say that I had nothing to do. Oxfam's approach to the vast problems of poverty and deprivation so exactly accords with many of the ideas I have expressed earlier, that it is possible for me to give time and energy to the local group with an almost total lack of mental reservations. These I might have about most other voluntary work, excepting perhaps only peace movement groups. The issues involved seem to me to be absolutely germane to the ultimate survival of any kind of acceptable existence for all of us on our planet,

Finally to ask oneself "If I had my time over again, would I have acted differently?" seems to me futile. Not only do we ourselves change and develop in response to circumstances; the social climate itself presents new demands and different restraints with each year that passes. We cannot unlearn what our individual lives have taught us, and thus cannot imagine with a mind unaffected by our experience and knowledge, how we might have acted differently.

What we can do is to build on those parts of our present being which seem to have positive, life-enhancing characteristics, and to disregard as far as possible the guilts, the regrets, the negations which we have accumulated by our mistakes. It is not so much a matter of counting one's blessings (a passive exercise at best) as of recognising that there is, because of all that has gone before, still a way forward.

For some years in my mind, and for many months in the setting down, I have struggled - largely in comparative isolation - to clarify for myself what I can identify with in our society of the eighties, and what I feel I must reject as regressive, unhelpful, insulting to the potential dignity of human beings.

Now, it is mostly written, and something rather startling is happening:

I am continually coming upon references (in newspapers, books, words of all kinds both factual and fictional, a considerable proportion of them written by women), which express ideas so similar to my own that I am in turn cast down and then exhilarated. Cast down because it would appear that I have had little original to say about anything; exhilarated by the realisation that there are obviously so many others "out there" who feel, think, aspire, conclude as I do about what seems important.

Any words of mine which are an expression of current feminist philosophy, derive from something within my own consciousness. Doubtless I have been influenced by the considerable exposure which the women's movement, the feminist lobby, the female liberation campaign - call it what you will - has received in the past few years. But I have not, I believe, written the majority of these chapters with that in the forefront of my mind and am obliged to conclude that some force hitherto unrecognised in most of us has released a new phenomenon in our society.

There must, then, be some kind of common consciousness spread about among a significant number of people, particularly women, who have never met, whose lives are quite differently structured, who do not necessarily read the same material or even live in the same society. I cannot accept that this phenomenon is simply attributable to the triumphs of modern mass communication, since such a theory does not allow for the effects of distortion, misinformation, propaganda or special pleading, all of which are inherent in every nation's media.

I am, rather, persuaded that there exists basic to the human condition, independent of all our widely differing cultures, classes, politics, social structures, a shared dream of how life might be.

For the first time in our history, perhaps some of us are finding in such a consciousness the courage to erect, in the harsh daylight of today's world, and with trembling hope, a skeleton framework around which our dream may one day be built.

I may have only a microscopically tiny contribution to make to the improvement of humankind's lot on this earth. I still have much to learn about how best that contribution can be made.

Rather than being totally cast down in contemplation of the world's hugely complex problems which seem often quite beyond solution, or wasting my remaining energies in profitless self-enquiry into my own puny and ephemeral uncertainties, I shall try to concentrate on the next stage of the journey.

I take with me the belief that my reflections have afforded me both resolve and resolutions, and in the heartening knowledge that I am one among a multitude with a common dream.

Hills

A childhood passed in the soft embrace
Of the gentle chalky Chiltern slopes:
On the close-cropped turf of that quiet place
I walked and talked and dared my hopes.
The skylark's song, the plover's call
My loveliest music. Scent of wild thyme,
Tiny bright flowers at each footfall -
Treasure past measure, all of it mine
To remember now, a lifetime on.

Northern hills, harder, their beauty stark
Ask a different love, a braver one
To carry with me into the dark.

The Chevin - Belper

The Chevin's gentle hills,
Like arms cradling the valley
Embracing the town,
Seem ever-changing
Yet ever constant.

Mist-wrapped or snow-capped,
Gale-torn or rain-stormed,
In sun or in shadow,
Their presence a joy.

From days long gone
The memories flow.
Walks in all weathers
Together, alone,
Sharing with children and friends
All the pleasures
And treasures held in those arms.

Now I watch as sunset's glory
Silhouettes the hills
And find a kind of peace.

Assignment Unfulfilled

At the beginning of each of our school terms, there was a task to be completed by teachers and pupils during the first lessons in each subject which many of us found irritating. In our "Assignment Books" we had to enter, at the teacher's dictation, the syllabus through which we would work during the coming weeks.

I normally disliked this custom particularly since it destroyed any element of surprise which might be awaiting us in the duller subjects. Our English Assignments, however, were a delight since they hinted at new treasures to be discovered before term ended, and as our English teacher was one of rare ability, I knew that I would never be disappointed by the quality of these discoveries.

It happened that one term, in our English Assignment Books, we wrote down, as usual, a list of titles for essays which we would write in that term. The first four had nothing to mark them as unusual. They were in the customary range of "My Hobby", "A Crowded Bus", or "Moving House". But the fifth title caused many of us to lift our pens and eyebrows. It was, simply, the word "Green". Miss E. refused with a smile to amplify it further, and we closed our Assignment Books and turned to the work of the term's first English lesson.

That term must have been a particularly busy one. Perhaps we were rehearsing for the annual play (always a great occasion at Christmas), or it may have been the summer term during which our final and gigantic Fête-for-the-Swimming-Bath-Fund took place.

At any rate I realised during our last English lesson that we had never reached the fifth essay title, "Green", and I was mildly disappointed. I wondered very much what Miss E. had in mind when she set the word down. And many, many times in the past twenty years, the little matter of that title has teased my mind.

Some two or three years after I had left school I was lying in a bluebell wood, my mind full of romantic dreams, and marvelling at the sun-lightened colours of the young beech leaves above my head. "Green thoughts in a green shade" indeed. Perhaps this was what Miss E. had been seeking? Certainly, she would have been disappointed at the unimaginative treatment I might have given to the subject at fifteen or sixteen; - I had half written the essay in my mind, on and off through that term - the delights of a smooth newly-mown lawn, the restful wash of a calm green sea, and so on.

During the war, the essay again came into my mind when I saw the perversion of green in its peaceful significance in the standard olive and khaki camouflage of factories, guns, military vehicles. Even in our own A.T.S. uniforms, the stockings were apt to change after several washings to a particularly unpleasant, bilious shade. This ugly transformation of colour might have made a bitter and unforeseen paragraph in my essay.

The years began to pass more quickly, and it was not until I learned of Miss E.'s death - I think it was just before the end of the war - that I thought again about that little unfulfilled task.

Did she, perhaps, intend or hope for a humorous treatment? Certainly "green" was a popular slang-word in the thirties (is it still?) for the stupid or uninitiated. Indeed, at parties, to the tune of "Auld Lang Syne" we used to chant "How green you are" to the victim in one version of Hunt the Slipper, instead of calling out "Hot" or "Cold" as he searched for his quarry.

I sometimes regret that I cannot hand in my piece of work on

"Green" now - I have so much more to say on the subject, though I should find it difficult to adhere to our rigid composition rule of "Introduction (preferably with quotation), Subject Para. 1, Subject Para. 2, Conclusion." At the most unlikely moments I find myself making mental notes from which to work on the essay.

Green - one of the few colours which refuses to look well on my small daughter, with her boisterous, fun-loving, generous nature; the discussion of the "suiting" of certain colours to certain personalities, apart from fashion or natural colouring , opens up a whole essay in itself.

Green - the muted, lovely oriental shade of my growing set of table-ware, each piece marking the passing of some anniversary, the celebration of a piece of good luck, or merely a burst of extravagance.

Green - the pale clean colour which, combined with a rich red, has transformed my formerly shabby kitchen into a working place of light and pleasantness. My delight in it (and my husband's!) is all the greater because this time I had a hand in the transformation, whereas with most of our other home-decorating, while the children were younger and more demanding, I could do little more than encourage, criticise and make cups of tea.

Green - the shaded glowing greenness which came from the lamp near our young son's bed during the nights of his first separation from us in a hospital ward. The misery and loneliness which were his part as he stared at the lamp we can only imagine, but knowing his temperament our imagination needed little prompting when he pointed out the green shaded light to us on the first visiting day.

After all, however, there is in the normal order of things

another half a lifetime of greenness to discover, before I can finally submit my essay. And when I do, I wonder if Miss E., among the initiated, will help me, a "green" one, to find my way about a little in that sphere where, tradition has it, the predominant colours are gold and white and blue.

Return Journey

Today I came in search of old Heart-lands
Travelling across half a century
Towards my Chiltern childhood.

Along this road
Chaperoned on after Chapel walks
By an old, silent, childless aunt
I found companionship
In the hippety-hopping skip
Of springy alder stick.
Home-bound, my temporary friend
- For Sunday decorum's sake -
Must be abandoned, at the bend
Where houses took over
From may-flower hedge.
(Bread-and-cheese trees, we called them,
Chewing on shiny leaves, pretending savour.)

Harebell and mignonette, alder and may
All now tidied away
Beneath twice-as-wide roaring highway.

Later, wilder more secret paths recall
Tentative explorations of first loves,
Where cowslip, briar rose and old man's beard
Were inspiration for poetic pledge
Of imagined constancy.

Today, white sign-boards posted at each end
Mark desecrated lanes: The Abbots' Walk
To Hilly Fields and Bull Pond Hollow
By way of Half Moon Rise:
All become Eighties suburbia to the life.
Last evening's lager-louts shampoo smart cars.
Sophisticated three-year-olds are clicked
Into safety harnesses ready for flight
To some ever-narrowing green belt.

Do any of these,
Catch echoes of our outcries of delight
That time we found an orchid hid in grass;
A dew-jewelled spider's web stretched between twigs?
Do they still hear the song of the meadow-lark
Her territory buried far below
Their tarmac drive, their flag-stone patio?

Waiting no answer I turn aside and climb
The gentle chalky slopes. And on the brow
Of this round hill I think of still as mine
I touch the turf and breathe the hint of thyme
And am appeased.

Up here I once knew star-bright visions;
Poured out my heart-aches to the thunder clouds;
Watched London burn in that first war-torn year;
Dreamed of what life might offer next. And here
Across the green downs
You came towards me bearing our shared future.

This place was Paradise when we were young.

April 1988

Winter Mo(u)rning

Night has been hard with unforgiving frost:
Black silence stressing everything that's lost
With your leaving.
And grieving
I walk the lonely meadows
In the misty rise of lemon winter sun.
So cold.
Yet with the morning still not old
The thaw's begun.
From hedge-tips and tree-fingers
And the white-bounden reeds,
Matching my tears
Fall tiny jewels, iridescent globes.
Each within its brilliance bears
(Too fragile for my grasp)
Some hint of hope, some pledge
From regions far beyond my understanding
That winter will not last.

1994

A Question

How to encompass the enormity of death?

A height, a depth, an impenetrable mass
Of emptiness remains.
Once filled with solid certainty
Of lover, closest friend,
A nullity - impossible to grasp, to hold,
Haunts every corner, every stair.
The oblivion of sleep is but the path
To the renewed pain of waking.

Time too throws down the challenge.
Once there were measured sections in each day,
Their ends and their beginnings filled
With gestures, words, looks, loving deeds -
Connections linking one hour to the next.
One life to another, yours to mine.
Now time has no end and no beginning,
The hour never to come when you return.
Your last "Hullo" was also your "Goodbye".

How to encompass the enormity of death?

1995

Subtraction and Addition

Time passes...
Now as the instant flash
Of the kingfisher's wing:
Now in slow march, aeons between each step.

Against the limitless minus of loss
I begin to set
An occasional plus.

Keeping you locked in memories
I seek positives outside of our oneness
Though the raw wound still bleeds.

Here is a paradox:
Because you are not here
To see the spring, to hear our music,
To greet our friends,
I seem to live with more awareness.
Inexplicably
Colours are subtly more lovely,
Sounds sharper, faces kinder
Than when my whole being
Was shared with yours.

In faltering moments of peace
Even sadness
Has wisps of poignant beauty.

So you have left me gifts
More than you could know.

But a plus can never equal a minus.

1995

Lessons

Someone said, witnessing my grief:
'Now you have surely known the very worst.
Nothing will ever hurt so much again.'
They spoke the truth. But, then I could not know
How long it would last, this unrelenting pain.

Others said: 'It never goes away,
But as with a lost or unsound limb
You learn acceptance.' They too told no lie.
This must be life's hardest, harshest lesson,
Though learning it still leaves the question: Why?

Yet with such learning something new's revealed:
Awareness that a greater mystery
Links every human spirit in one chain.
We may not ever be completely healed,
But we can share the siblinghood of pain.

1996

On the Passing of the Years

Now I must learn acceptance
Of the passing of the years.

My feet still tap to those rhythms
And itch to join the dance.
But wishing is not all:
Knee joints moved freely
Breathing came easily
The spine was supple
And stamina had no end.

Now aching lies not simply in the bones
The heart too is heavy with weight of loss.

Weeping at the beauty of a song
That sings me back to earlier, joyful times,
I think I shall not dance, nor sing again,
But I will remember and be glad
And try to be content.

May 1997

So Many Things...

So many things not done
So many things unsaid
And some words spoken that should not have been.

Even after so long such thoughts disturb,
Increase the yearning for some miracle reversal
That we both might make amends.

The knowing that all who've ever grieved
Have walked this way
Affords scant comfort.

Only deep within
My unbelief is tempted into hope
That maybe, just maybe
You somehow know, and forgive
As I long since forgave you
For leaving.

June 1997

In the Bookshop

I had thought
The poems of loss were all done with,
All grief written out. But no.

Here, in the calm of a book-store,
From a small well-fashioned volume
The cover portrait of its subject -
One John Harrison, Clockmaker -
Stares up at me.

Now time itself stops.
I reach for the story, thinking:
"This, for you, will be a perfect gift."

We once saw his work in Greenwich:
A man after your own heart,
Yorkshire born, self-taught,
Living forty years with his obsession
To find the perfect time-piece.
"A lone genius," reads the blurb,
"Who solved the greatest scientific problem of his time."

But of course
No-one has stopped the clocks.

Replacing the book
I close my eyes
To hide the glisten of tears
That will form the well-spring of these lines.

December 1998

Jean's Story

I scrambled down over the tailboard of an Army transport truck into a day that changed my life. It was 1943.

The outbreak of war four years earlier had already changed hundreds of thousands of lives with every day that had passed, but this was one which I would always remember with a slight sense of unbelief. Could this really be happening to me?

We had been travelling in some discomfort since before dawn and had now arrived at a secret destination deep in the Buckinghamshire countryside.

My kitbag was thrown down to me and with my companions I stumbled, still half asleep, towards a sentry box beside high iron gates leading into parkland. We presented our passes.

I don't recall that any code words had to be exchanged. Minutes later I had become a tiny cog in that complex construction known as Station X, to be revealed many years later as the war time code-breaking centre.

Since leaving school, I had worked as a trainee journalist, an audit clerk and most recently as secretary to the chief engineer of a company engaged in producing such unexciting artifacts as oil filters and spark plugs for the war machine.

I had volunteered some months previously to join the services and now, after many delays, interviews, tests and vetting I was in the Auxiliary Territorial Service which was later to become known as the Women's Royal Army Corps.

Madam,

    I am directed to refer to your letter dated 16th
September, 1943 and to say that the Ministry of Labour
have been instructed by this Department to send you to, No.7
A.T.S. Training Centre for preliminary training. As the
Adjutant of the Training Centre is fully aware of the
nature of the duties for which you have been selected it
will not be necessary for you to take any letters of
acceptance etc., with you.

    I am,
      Madam,
        Your obedient Servant,

John F. Natt

Director of Military Intelligence.

Miss J.L. Darby,
  Warden House,
    Downs Road,
      Dunstable,
        Beds.

Following initial training and a short course in the mysteries
of radio signalling I had been drafted as a member of the
Intelligence Corps to Bletchley Park.

As we were marched towards our billets, I tried to take in
some of the features of this country estate that was soon to
become a familiar environment to me.

Trees, a lake, well-kept grassy stretches and here and there
incongruous single-storey structures similar to many that had

arisen since 1939. And overlooking all, an imposing mansion through whose doors a stream of people were coming and going, some in high-ranking military uniforms, others in casual civvies.

Later, settling into the camp before starting work, I was confronted with the first indication of the kind of company I was now to encounter on a daily basis.

"What did you read?" asked the beautiful blonde lounging on the camp bed next to mine.

"Sorry?" My mind was a blank. Did she expect a run-down of my favourite authors?

"When were you up?" she continued.
"Up where?"

"Which university were you at?"

A light flashed through the fog of my ignorance. "Oh. Sorry. I left school at 16. Haven't had any higher education."

There was a brief silence and then, surprisingly, I was accepted without further question into the charmed circle around me as though this distinction was of no consequence at all. We had all been selected, whatever our backgrounds, as being able to cope with what lay ahead. And from that day, I was to experience a period of ever-growing awareness of the infinite variety of human life stories.

The following morning I began my first shift of duty as a cipher clerk.

Now that many of the secrets of Station X have been made the subject of books, television programmes, open days and talks for the general public, it is hard to believe that we had all sworn never in our lifetimes to divulge details of what we heard, saw, learned or did during our time at Bletchley Park.

Even the closest members of our families had to be met with determined prevarication when they asked, out of sheer interest in the progress of the war, "What exactly is it that you are doing there?"

Indeed, apart from those at the top who were privy to the objectives of the whole enterprise, most of us were not aware even of what was happening in the huts adjacent to our own work-stations and we never discussed our duties outside of those huts or asked others what they were doing.

Much less did we know of what happened to the results of our daily tasks. What we were made to realise was the great importance of each individual's contribution to the ultimate success of whatever the operation was.

But it was not the work alone which made the time at Bletchley so mind-expanding. The mixture of backgrounds of people working there meant that the choice of how to spend leisure time was almost bewildering.

For instance, we could go boating on the lake and when on night shift it was an especially magical sensation to do this during our midnight break, gently circling the little island in the moonlight and disturbing the resident flock of Canada geese.

Apart from the usual range of sporting activities - including some variations introduced by our American cousins - there were such pastimes as chess, singing, drama, concerts, bridge, discussion groups - the list went on and on.

And within some of these circles were those who were experts in their fields, professional actors, a radio announcer, trained musicians, science graduates, and with any or all of them one could mix and learn. Indeed, after the war I realised that my years at Bletchley had been for me the equivalent of a university course.

An unorthodox higher education it may have been, but a richly cultural time nevertheless. On a brief return for a reunion a few years back, it seemed to me that that wartime period had been experienced by another person than myself.

So many subsequent days that changed my life have come and gone - marriage, the birth of children, bereavements - that looking back to the 1940s was like remembering a dream sequence. But without Bletchley my life history would have been very different.

On that return to the park, I would have liked to find out what had happened to some of those with whom I had shared such a significant part of my youth, but of course many of them were not there to ask. Most of them would have been in their seventies and eighties or have long since died.

Did the young man who planned to train for the priesthood, not from a sense of vocation but as a secure livelihood, make a success of it and live happily with his conscience?

Did staying on to join the post-war establishment in GCHQ at Cheltenham prove to be a satisfying choice for some of my ex-colleagues?

Is the young woman who espoused Christian Science, refusing all medication for various ailments still alive and well? Which of the numerous romances begun in Station X endured? My own ended on return to the realities of civilian life.

Some of those I worked alongside became, in their post-war lives, public figures: a cabinet minister, professors in a number of disciplines, a famous historian, a musicologist and composer, more than one actor. Interestingly most of these success stories relate to men. As far as I am aware, few of the brilliant women working at Bletchley have achieved public acclaim.

There was little hope of following the peacetime stories of those glamorous other worldly beings from the U.S., with their immaculately tailored uniforms, their wealth, their sophistication, or of those less flamboyant allies from a number of European countries who had joined the establishment.

All part of that dream-like time, they evaporated into their new lives. I wonder - do any of them ever wonder what happened to me?

After The Cataract

Daily I search for words
To celebrate the wonders of my new-washed
world
Of detail, form and colour.

Sharp edges of trees stand clear
Against growing light of morning sky.
As though from an inner energy source
Chrome taps sparkle.
Glass tumblers, fresh from rinsing
Laugh - radiant with rays
Of reflected brightness.

But the colours!
The world's aflame with a brilliance
I had forgotten.
I marvel, as when seeing revealed
The painting of an Old Master
Stripped by a skilled conservator
Of the varnish and grime of centuries.

So in one half-hour
Another expert cleared the clouding cataract
And brought me back lost beauties.

November 2000

Love Poem at 80

Love?
Haven't I always known
What love is?

Mother, father, brother,
Janet, a ginger-haired doll.
Teacher, object of schoolgirl passion.
Film-star worshipped from afar.
First secret embraces...

For all of these
I used, mis-used
That overworked, treacherous,
Significant, indispensable word.

Awaited my lifetime's love.

Today my house overflowed
Family and friends
Joining with the spirits
Of those far away,
Of those no longer earth-bound
All, all telling, whispering,
Laughing, crying their love.

So after eight decades
I find that love
Is forever unfolding new truths.

Love?
It's indefinable
But more real than the solid earth
Or the distant sky.

June 3rd 2001

Envy

Envy was a stranger
To a life rich in love,
Friendship, music
And the satisfaction of knowledge gained.

But suddenly challenging
Came, as if for the first time,
Awareness of the beauty of the young;
The perfection of straight toes
Bared to the world in sandals;
The startling agility of cricketers
Leaping, rolling, running,
The hopes of lovers with a future.
And envy walked in their shadow
Demanding recognition.

Yet I too once slid down banisters,
Ran barefoot through wet grass
In sheer sensual delight,
Knew energy unbounded,
Chose clothes to grace, not hide my shape.

While adding to experience
Age, thief-like,
Steals from us day by day
Much that makes us whole,
Forcing a never-ending fight
Against vain regrets.

For who envies the old,
Except, perhaps, the dead?

September 2002

Biking

There was a time long years ago
When two wheels took me far and wide.
My cycle, almost part of me
Was always there for me to ride.

A group of schoolmates formed a club -
Black and white pennants on handlebars.
We toured the county each weekend,
Keeping to by-ways empty of cars.

Time passed, and still I rode my bike,
But left my schoolmates far behind.
A different mate rode with me now
For adventures of a different kind!

With picnics packed in saddlebags
We went exploring east and west,
Seeking out churches, ancient ruins,
Bluebell woods - my life was blest.

Time went on passing. Lifestyles changed.
Cycling neglected for many a year,
Until retirement day arrived
Bringing another change of gear.

My leaving gift - a shiny bike.
I took delivery with pleasure
And rode it home, aglow with thoughts
Of how I'd enjoy this latest treasure.

Alas, how stupid had I been
To think of touring Derbyshire
On my two shiny gleaming wheels
When I was in my sixtieth year!

Dodging traffic on the busy A6
The least of problems I would face,
But all those hills on either side
Must be climbed to reach almost any place.

Before long my treasure began to rust
And I decided that it must go.
So I sold it, regretfully. Now I ride
Only my memories of long ago.

June 2003

On Learning To Be Old

It's far from easy
Learning to be old -
Not just elderly -
Definitively old.
You thought it would just happen,
Hoped that you'd cope -
That mind and body would hold.

Then you begin to wonder if you're seen
As little old lady, or proverbial sheep
Posing as lamb.
(Dress too brightly and you risk looking cheap;
Too quietly in beige crepe de chine,
Identity fades to a microgram.)
Put on weight - can you blame the pills?
Shrink to skin and bone - is this that worst of all ills?

But there's more to OLD than all that.
You'd not bargained for the fact
That to many, OLD is invisible.
On crowded pavements you're edged aside.
In a queue
It seems that others
Have more important things to do
Than you.

Hardest of all is learning
To manage the inner part:
You wonder about roads not taken;
Where other old ones have gone.
You mustn't stand still, feel forsaken,
Nor wallow in old wounds, lost loves,
Undying longings of the flesh and heart -
Sometimes the effort seems almost too great.
But you keep moving, although it's so late.

It's far from easy
Learning to be old.

September 2003

A Weekend with Mozart

On a magic carpet of music
We rode in two days
Through Mozart's last ten golden years.

Led by an expert, empathetic,
We travelled in and out of that troubled world,
Now feeling the pain of many hardships,
Now stunned anew by a transcendent beauty,
Hearing darkness, dazzled by brilliance,
The outpouring of his genius a constant wonder
So that when at last we left behind
The sorrow and the sweetness that was Mozart
We carried with us rich and lasting treasures.

November 2003

Paradox

When the tide of memory
Seems to be ebbing
Sometimes a rogue wave rises
To swamp the present
Before receding to leave in its wake
Vivid structures from the past -
A scene, a song, a phrase
Long-forgotten, now fleetingly recovered
Before once again the shore is empty
And memory struggles with nostalgia.

December 2003

A Different Kind of Grief

After ten years alone
There comes peace - of a kind -
A final acceptance of loss.

So it is, for much of the time.
But a different kind of grief
Not born of loneliness or longing
Can still overwhelm.

Delight in a shaft of sunshine
Lighting on winter aconites;
The notes of Isolde's Liebestod
Haunting the day's end;
The glimpse of an old stone building
Caught from a train window -
Such may be triggers for tears
Because you are missing all these
And much, much else
That we would have shared in love.

Then the carefully nurtured covering
Around my heart
Is pierced again and again
So that in each moment of my joy
It bleeds a little
And the truths in some old fairy tales
Are made flesh.

March 2004

Daisy-Chains

I sit by the river
Idly starting a daisy-chain -
But my daughter
Is now full grown
With a child of her own -
A boy who'd not thank me
For such an odd fancy...

So instead I recall
Daisy-chains of my childhood
Then those we made together
When she was still small.

Now, as wild flowers should not be culled
I'll pick no more daisies.
Just watch the river
Flow silently by, fast,
Like time itself as it bleeds into the past.

September 2004

Missing Memories

The store-room, dim-lit, cold,
As shadowy as those memories
Missing when they handed over
Her clothes, old letters, cards,
A few pieces of jewelry -
Nothing of value. For us
The most precious things were gone:
Her photo albums.
Had the Care Home burned them?
Tossed them in a bin?
No-one knew - or if they did,
They weren't admitting it.

Now all I have are flickering memories
Of faded snapshots - a poignant tiny part
Of a family's life experience.
My mother in late youth stands proud,
Hand up to rich dark chignon of hair
High-throated dress, waspwaisted.
Her wedding: women in stiff long gowns,
Wide-brimmed hats and elbow-length white gloves.
Men even more buttoned-up
Wing collars and grease-plastered hair.
Then my father and an uncle
Self-conscious in the khaki uniform
Of World War One - peaked caps and smart puttees.

And later, father, mother and small boy
Walking on a seaside promenade,
My brother's age telling me
I was not yet born
When my father wore plus-fours
And my mother a deep-crowned cloche hat.

Like half-remembered dreams
Those missing albums haunt consciousness -
My family ghosts, tantalising...

October 2004

Beth's Poetry Trail

Jean was a very active member of the steering Group formed to create a poetry trail in Belper following the death of Beth Fender who founded the two poetry groups in the town.

Jean wrote a booklet about the trail, "Beth and Belper - Tale of a Trail", which describes the many meetings the group held over a five year period and some of the struggles involved in creating the trail.

One of the poems on the trail was written by Jean.

Words on a Wall

As builders, fashioning a wall,
Create beauty in strength,
Shaping each stone
To fit snugly with its neighbour,
So a poem, each word honed,
May shape a message
Of inner strength and calm
For a troubled world.

August 2005

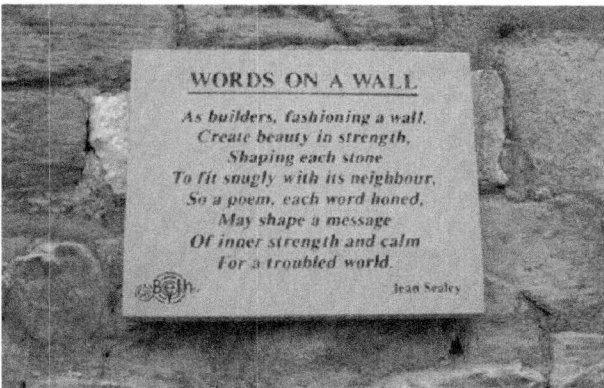

Beth's Poetry Trail Poem

Because she loved poetry,
Knew what it could offer
In so many parts of life,
She wanted to share that love and knowledge
With any who would accept her gift.
Now we, who loved her,
Want to pass on that offering
To you.

As you pass by
Stay for a moment -
Read and be enriched
By what poems can give you -
Joy, courage, solace, insight, laughter -
Beth's trail is for you.

Some Reflections on a Pre-War Childhood

1921-1939 - but that's history! Yes, the beginnings of MY history - a childhood that now seems idyllic, almost a fantasy world when viewed in the context of today.

Home was an in-between-the-wars end-of-terrace house in what was then a small market town, lying in a gap in the Chiltern Hills, where two old Roman roads, Watling Street and the Icknield Way, crossed. So another, far older history than mine was all around me, brought dramatically to life on one occasion when an archaeological dig unearthed skeletons in one of the mounds on " The Downs" .

Much later, in my early teens romantic period I would imagine a handsome bronze-skinned youth from the distant past living in a secret cavern beneath those hills and I would write a love-story based on his survival as the remaining member of his race. The word "bronze" somehow seeped from the metal into my idea of a pre-historic person.

But to return to my earliest years: memories naturally lie almost exclusively in and around the house and garden. Dolls, of course, played a significant role in my life. Among them was Janet, whose ginger hair I treasured because to me she was unique - I had yet to encounter any human redheads. I was to be introduced to the emotion of grief early, when my life-sized baby doll, with blue eyes that opened and shut, fell from my embrace and her china head shattered. Tragedy!

However she was sent away to the Dolls' Hospital (do such places still exist, I wonder?) "for an operation" and came back with her head miraculously whole again. I can summon the feel of that china surface beneath my fingers to this day.

Her pram was a rather odd shade of khaki, but I loved it and was proud as punch when I took Janet and my baby out in it for walks.

There were few cars to cause much danger on the roads then. The milk was delivered in metal churns carried on a horse-drawn cart, the milkman measuring it out into our jugs from half-pint and pint ladles. Groceries came in a basket on the front of Mr. Holton's bicycle.

Street lamps were gas-lit and I used to watch at dusk for the lamp-lighter to come with his long pole, lifting it to the lantern shapes at the top of the iron posts, and as if by magic the lights would come on.

There was an occasion when the road past our house was covered with straw and I seem to remember being told that it was to deaden the sound of the black-plumed horses' hooves and the wheels of the carriages of a funeral cortege, because one of our neighbours was lying gravely ill in bed.

Our front garden was small, with a low wall surmounted by decorative iron railings, and was entered by means of a matching iron gate. (All this metal would disappear in 1940 - to help the war effort, so we were told.) My father took pride in keeping this front garden neatly planted. A grass plot surrounded the circular central bed which bloomed unvaryingly every spring with scarlet tulips in a frame of blue forget-me-nots.

Attached to the back of the house was a brick-built shed which for some part of my childhood became my house. I would regularly sweep the cobbled floor, wash the little window, hang up remnants of net curtaining and arrange wild flowers in jam-jars.

Mother occasionally even let me have my dinner there on a

fine day. I blissfully ignored the fact that a large heap of household coal was stored in one corner of my living-room.

From a patterned slate-tiled yard a path led under a rustic wooden arch into the back garden, passing on the way a small patch of soil which my brother and I were encouraged to use for our own horticultural experiments. Beyond, the main garden which then seemed to me huge, though it was actually quite limited. A lawn, two side borders and at the far end a bed filled with phlox plants. I loved sucking the nectar from the little blossoms in season.

In spring there were always tulips somewhere in that garden. I once asked my mother what made the little black spots in the base of each bloom and she told me they were the footprints of tulip fairies who played there at night. One could at that time buy folding paper photographic souvenirs from seaside resorts. When closed these measured about one by one-and-a-half inches. One evening I left one such "letter" in one of the tulips for the fairies. I was overjoyed next morning to discover that it had gone. When I grew up and recalled this and countless other instances of her imagination I realised what a wonderful infant teacher my mother would have made.

Lifting the latch and going through the back gate you would find a fenced-in patch of bare soil. At some stage this was used as a hen-run, but when there were no hens there I remember commandeering it as my cowboy ranch, complete with bunk-house. I must have been looking at my brother's comics! When there were hens in residence and laying, spare eggs were preserved in an enamel bucket of ising-glass. I disliked intensely having to retrieve them from the slithery solution when we ran out of fresh ones.

Leaving the hen-run behind and passing along the backs of adjoining houses another path led into "The Lane", and then to the churchyard and cemetery of the ancient Priory church. This area was rumoured to be haunted by Sally the Witch and was a place to be avoided after dark.

There were never any instances of physical punishment from either of our parents, although we must sometimes have tried their patience sorely. My father could be stern but never lifted his hand to strike us. My mother was the soul of serenity. So much so that I can remember only one occasion when we must have exasperated her beyond endurance. I don't know what we had done to cause her to say, totally un-characteristically, that she was leaving us, but she walked out of the front door, hat and coat on and suitcase in hand. My tears and my brother's desperate shouts must have brought her back, for of course she didn't go far. I can only hope that her action resulted in angelic behaviour on our part, at least for a time, though here my memory does fail me.

At the age of ten my environment expanded when I began to travel daily by bus to the "big girls'" school in a neighbouring town, and towards what are now called the teenage years. But that's a story for another time perhaps.

November 2005

Echoes of the Flow of Time

Eight decades lived
And Time's perspective's changed.
In all those long years
There was only the present
Or bright anticipation of a future.

Now echoes from the past
Course down Time's rivers
Bringing scherzos of laughter
Lamentos of pain
Tremolos of fear -
Cherished voices calling, rising, falling,
Fading into silence.

Today's future is a threnody,
Its echo one of not-quite-fear -
Rather of unknowing...
Can what has not yet been
Send back an echo?

February 2006

Another Spring

One October
Dylan had his "thirtieth year to heaven".
This Spring
In my eighty-fourth year earth-given
I gaze again in wonder
At the miracle of the trees' greening
In hues without number.

Near and far
Are marvels of structure and design -
Statuesque, thrusting, weeping;
Feathery, bushy, stencilling the air,
Their myriad greens a delight,
Accentuated here and there
By effervescent blossom, pink and white.

And here outside my window
My magnolia - love-gift from a long-ago day
Flaunts its thousand creamy cups
For a brief display
Before its own greening spills them down.
I know that next October must bring
The turning of greens to copper, bronze and brown,
But I will have seen another Spring.

May 2006

Transformation

The wartime bride
Smiles with pride
Beside her young husband
On leave for his wedding
In ceremonial "blues*.

Later, she's a happy mother,
Her bubbly daughter
Laughing up at her father -
My brother.

Then the full life
Of busy housewife -
Member of choirs, musical theatre,
Canal-boat holidays
Journeys abroad
To visit the much-travelled daughter.

But time brings change -
A gradual winding-down,
The occasional frown
When memory fails to arrange
The right words in order.

Then the years as they pass
Take away, all unseen,
More parts of that mind
Once whole and serene.

But what of the husband
After sixty shared years?
His caring's now of a different kind
As he tends the woman
The shade of his wife -
Almost a stranger
Mostly absent, though still by his side.

I weep for them both
And curse the unfairness of life.

November 2006

Some Further Reflections on a 1920's Childhood

I began school life in a tiny kindergarten-type establishment two doors away from home. It was run by a middle-aged lady and her daughter. There were about 15 to 20 of us in the school, all ages from five to ten years old. Some of the most vivid memories I have of this time include the younger woman introducing us to the French language. I don't know what qualifications she could possibly have had for this, but we learned to count by repeating after her "un", "deux" (do, as we say), "trois", "quatre" (the soft-furred pet), "cinque" (what the ship did) "six" (like when we say stop), "sept" (what jelly does when cold), etc. etc. However, I still remember some of the French nursery rhymes she taught us !

We often climbed the Downs, two main hills forming part of the Chiltern range. My brother and I used to go up when the members of the London Gliding Club, which had its headquarters at the base of one hill, were launching their craft. In those early days of silent flight a team used to run with huge elasticated launching ropes from the plateau at the top of the hill until the glider reached the edge of what we called The Pit, the ropes then dropped away from their retaining hooks and the glider lifted into the thermals and away across the countryside.

The Pit was also the scene at Easter for the Orange Rolling ceremony. Did this have its roots in the old tradition of egg-rolling elsewhere in the country? I never discovered the origin of this custom.

There were always parties on birthdays, sometimes in our homes and sometimes in local halls. I can still remember one or two of the presents given to me on one such occasion. It was my first really big party, held in the public room of a local pub-cum-hotel. I even know who gave me the miniature square handbag covered in a mock-suede material in stripes of light mauve and deep purple. His name was George and he was the son of the greengrocers in the High Street.

My childhood was always filled with music. Both parents belonged to the town's amateur musical-dramatic society and performed as well in concerts as soloists. The chapel had a tradition of presenting an oratorio every year, in which professional nationally famous singers took the solo part. My brother played the saxophone and drums in local orchestras and dance bands, and we 'had a wind-up gramophone and a small collection of shellac records which had pride of place in the front room.

The piano lived in the drawing room and we could all play it with varying degrees of skill - mine being the least, as I found reading music very difficult and preferred to find my own way into a tune by ear. Mother also played the mandolin - that seems to me now a quite exotic accomplishment. When I was old enough in my early teens I joined the chapel choir and became moderately proficient at sight-reading. I doubt I could even manage the simplest tune at sight now.

My father's eldest sister spent Christmas with us once. She was known for her endless talking, and nothing would stop her once she was launched into a story. We had finished the first course of our Christmas meal, and Mother had passed round dishes of apple pie. Aunt reached across for the sugar caster (an essential on the table in those days), went on talking and we couldn't prevent her from taking up the pepper-pot by mistake, as she shook it liberally over her pie and custard. Even then she finished the story before asking for a fresh portion!

We lived next door to an elderly lady with two young-ish daughters, spinsters who also sang in local choirs and concerts. When my brother had to go into hospital one time, my parents left me in the charge of these women who naturally had little experience of looking after children. They spoiled me greatly. Of that visit two memories stand out - one was my fascination with their milk jug - a tiny article in the shape of a cow with a tail looped to make the handle and an open mouth from which they poured the milk. The other memory is that they introduced me to rice pudding containing juicy sultanas, a complete novelty. I haven't thought of that for eighty years!

Washdays were a major event each week. Always on a Monday. Mother would get up very early to light the fire under the copper in the back kitchen. There were no washing machines or other automatic aids, and the mangle was hand-turned with its wooden rollers. By the time we got up the water would be boiling and mother would be agitating the clothes in the soap-flaked water of the tub with a posser - a long-handled stick with a metal cup-shaped plate on the base.

Dinner-time would produce cold sliced meat from the Sunday joint, with mashed potatoes, possibly followed by a milk pudding. One time she had changed from rice to sago. I hated it, refused to eat it. She said I'd not get down until I'd done so. We both stuck it out until I could tell I had no choice, took a reluctant spoonful and found that what had revolted me when hot was quite acceptable cold, so that contretemps ended happily.

That generation of women worked terribly hard in the home. Washday always brought clouds of steam and if it was fine, a heavy load to be carried outside to be hung on propped-up clothes lines. On wet days the bed-linen and clothing had to be hung up on overhead racks or draped on wooden clothes-horses in front of the coal-fired kitchen range which was kept shiny with black-lead polish each week.

I remember our first vacuum-cleaner, a heavy cylindrical model almost too heavy to lift, but at least it replaced the Ewbank carpet sweeper that had to be emptied after every use, otherwise the contents just kept spilling out. Carpets were lifted in spring and heaved onto the clothes-line in the garden, to be heartily attacked with a wicker-work carpet sweeper.

Back to laundry tasks - on the day after washday, piles of damp ironing awaited. No electric irons then, heavy flat-irons which had to be heated over the kitchen range. There were always two, one heating up again while the other was being used. Everything was ironed, no drip-dry fabrics to ease the task. Learning to cope with stiff collars and cuffs on shirts was vital, and of course many items had to be starched, and white linens had been dipped in Robin blue-bag solution to maintain their pristine freshness.

More Thoughts on Aging

It doesn't occur
To the young and strong
Dancing along
In the joys of youth
Even to think about being old.

When middle-age arrives
A sober truth
Fills the days
With getting and achieving
Some stability to life.

Then suddenly, it seems,
Everyone's leaving
The certainties behind
And the future's shrinking.

Then comes the time
For some serious thinking
About the positives that are still around.
Sure, many negatives are lurking
To tempt bouts of self-pity
But it's a case of working
To stop them dragging you down.

For the old do have compensations -
Like the shrinking of temptations,
And there's much to be said
For a long lie in bed
While the outside world hurries
To the new day and its worries.
There's comfort, too, in the thought
That though sometimes it's fraught
Old age might be preferred
To being interred!

March 2007

Manuscript for the Writers Group

Intended to be neither morbid nor melancholy, I have put together some of the thoughts and reflections I have now that I am over halfway between my eighth and ninth decade.

Often when I'm performing routine chores, memory throws up forgotten snatches of conversations from long ago. I ask myself why these particular examples at this moment? Are they in fact truly random, or have they significance for me at the time they occur? Is my subconscious trying to tell me something?

Thinking about being a survivor among erstwhile contemporaries takes one down many by-ways. Why me? How long will I continue to be a survivor? Would I rather have preceded them than be left adrift on what can seem so often a very lonely path?

At 78, my father, seemingly contented to be spending his last years with my mother in a retirement home 100 miles away from the town they had lived in all their married life, and where he had held responsible offices, said quietly to me, on one of my last visits:

"I'd like to go back just once more to see the old familiar places."

Hearing his voice clearly in my head after nearly 30 years gave rise to all kinds of emotions and longings, for example to re-visit places that had been of significance to me.

When, therefore, I face the reality of the gradual diminution of my own opportunities for travel, for trying new experiences, for re-visiting cherished places, many so recently within walking distance, I have to repeat this mantra over and over:

I've been there, I've done that, I've had chances and taken them. Now I must live in memories, but still try to learn something each day.

When my mother, widowed, on her last visit to our home, said to my mother-in-law who had lived with us for eight years (that in itself was for me an enormous learning curve which I won't enlarge on here!)

"We've lived too long, haven't we, Clare?"

I found this hard to understand. I know now something of what she was feeling.

A very dear friend, knowing that she was dying, and being a very organised and caring person, calmly planned all the details of her funeral, even down to where the expected car drivers could park. This, she did, in order to relieve her family of at least some of what they would have to deal with, without her help.

One of the last things she said to us (on the last occasion of her visit to our home) was:

"I don't want to leave you all. And I just can't imagine not being here..."

Every time I recall this moment I realise that the time will come when I shall share those feelings.

Now in order to stave off morbidity, melancholy, even depression - my solution is to try to concentrate on all the pluses I've been allotted - the childhood maxim of count your blessings, perhaps? Chief among them are the waves of love and affection flowing from family and friends, and the consolation that although every day my body reminds me that

I'm no longer young and fit, at least I'm still relatively mobile, if slow, and above all that my mind is in reasonable working order.

All this may seem to you an odd offering for a manuscript evening of a writers' group, but I submit it for two reasons. Firstly, that this group has, and has always had from the very start, an atmosphere of empathetic acceptance of whatever its members choose to offer. Also that in offering this particular, perhaps eccentric piece, some of you may, one day, when you yourselves are entering true old age, recall something from this contribution and find help or comfort from it. Thank you.

September 2007

Learning To Let Go

It's a lifetime of learning -
The lessons never end.

Your parents -
Always there for you -
Die, and you have to let go.

Your first born starts school -
Goes through the gate
Without a backward glance.
Then you know there'll always be
A part of his life
Where you don't belong.
You will have to let go.

Years go by
Dreams fade in the light of reality.
The book you didn't get published,
The cruise on Norway's fjords
Prefaced always by "One day"
That never dawned.
Let it go.

So gradually
The discipline of letting go is learned
Except for the greatest loss.

And here's a paradox:
Though I believe
That I have let go -
The non-presence clings on -
One lesson forever unlearned.

February 2008

If I Could Write Music

I'd begin with the wind's
Soft sighing through tall grasses,
Slowly rising to a roaring crescendo
As it reaches the tree-tops.

Rhythms would be inspired
By the syncopated patter of raindrops
Or the gentle scudding of clouds
Across a summer sky.

The crack of thunder
And the drumming of hailstones
On shed roofs -
A perfect percussion section.

Then with the humming of bees
For the bass notes
And for melodies the rippling
Of the river over stones...

Oh! I'd give you songs
Sonatas and symphonies ---

If I could write music!

May 2008

Scent of Roses

I catch the scent of our roses
On June's clear burnished air
And am back in another summer
When we were waiting there
In that unkind ward with its warnings
Of what might still be to come.
I told you how lovely the roses were
That year, that I hoped you'd be home
In time to enjoy them in their prime.
"You go now, enjoy them," you said,
Smiling your gentle, generous smile
As I turned and left that hospital bed.

Now each year as the roses bloom
There's bitter-sweetness in their perfume.

A Second Coming

In Spring, the magnolia tree
Surpassed itself
With a thousand proud, blushing blooms.
They came early
In these out-of-kilter climate times.
And no frosts came to burn off
Those graceful, waxy cups.
For weeks they gave delight
Before throwing down
Their strangely hard, unlovely seeds
To rattle in the mower
Where grass had been their temporary bed.
Then the leaves, strong, rich and green
Made havens for mating birds
While the tree grew ever taller and thicker.
In its giantism it threatened wall
And all surrounding growth -
Perhaps even its own strength.
So in high summer came the surgeons
For a life-saving pruning.
Afterwards, without warning
Towards summer's end, unprecedented,
Came a startle of new blossoms
Each cradled in its leafy nest -
As they never were in spring
When branches are bare and brown.

Was this second coming a warning
Of other strange changes in the natural world?

But for now
With more than eighty Springs behind me
And no second coming in my philosophy,
I rejoice to watch my magnolia
Dipping its blossomed arms
In the passing breeze.

August 2008

In Mrs. Stott's School

It was called a kindergarten.

And it was only three doors away from our house. This was the nineteen-twenties. But as happens when you get old all your yesterdays are clearer than last week. And so I remember Mrs. Stott and her daughter Mildred, better than I can recall some of my own relatives.

Mrs. Stott and Mildred must have been trained in some way - Or weren't there such regulations then? There was an official Education Committee's school about a quarter of a mile away, where my brother (six years my senior) had his first lessons. Perhaps my parents had found it a bit too rough for me - I don't know. I never asked them why I went to Mrs. Stott's - as it was known.

There were two rooms in an ordinary detached house, a conservatory where we hung our coats and changed our shoes, and a garden with a croquet game on the lawn.

I presume I must have been taught reasonably efficiently since I learned very quickly to read, write and "do sums". Mildred also taught us a little French, though I don't know how she had come by that knowledge. I only recall that she used a dreadful sort of rhyming rote to teach us to count in that tongue - for example, "un" like "run", "deux" = "do", "trois" (this I forget), "quatre" was "like your pet cat", and - most memorable of all - "cinque" was "what ships did in a bad storm", - and so on.

Luckily for the equivalent of the 11+ exam to get into a grammar school, we didn't need oral French! We also learned that "all of the red bits on the map of the world belonged to us"!

Most of my memories as you might expect, are about my fellow pupils and their doings. A girl called Kathy, who often misbehaved and had what would now be recognised as special needs, - she frequently ate rubber erasers and licked the ink off the nib of her pen. When punished by the customary "stand in the corner with your back to the room", she would studiously lick the dark red wallpaper until she had managed to make a pale pink patch.

I suppose that because both Mrs. Stott and Mildred were their own bosses, and as far as I know were not subject to anything resembling today's Ofsted inspection, the school was a happy, gentle place, where we enjoyed what we were expected to do, and so learned easily. And when the change came for me to go to "the big School" which was five miles away and involved a bus journey and having to stay for lunch, and accept what must have seemed a rigid, rather stern regime it took me more than a year to adapt, and to get through each day without shedding a few tears.

Written May 2009

In England Now

Sometimes I feel
I am a traveller in a strange land -
A wanderer
Adrift from all that was once
Treasured, loved, familiar.

Mine was a world
Of quiet green fields, village ponds,
Wildflower meadows
And woods full of windflowers and shy white violets.

Fluffy clouds once made pictures
To stir the imagination.
Now the sky also hosts thin straight lines
That follow a ceaseless drone
Companion to the crowded roads below.
Once gentle horse-and-trap country.

Now I inhabit this alien world of technology
That I cannot love, but neither can I leave
Since it enfolds me quite, for better or worse.
A world where names deceive:
Websites aren't homes for spiders.
The internet doesn't keep hair tidy.
Supermarkets replace corner shops and penny bazaars.
Push-button controls no chance to rejoice
At the welcome sound of a human voice.

And yes, I know it's old age
But at least I once lived
In that world so different from yours,
And if I could just wave a Wand
I'd like to take you
To that old peaceful place
For just an hour or two
So that you could know
The England I once knew.

June 2009

January 1st 2000

From the clear blue arc
Of a rain-washed sky
Bright sun splashes sparkles of diamonds
Along the swollen rolling river.

Pealing bells are silenced
Midnight's noisy fireworks spent.
Revellers sleep exhausted
Missing this fresh new morning.

Peace is here in the valley
Where slender bare tree trunks
Reach tall up to the light.

Such quiet beauty
Celebrates for me this first day
More potently than all the strivings
Of the world's manufactures.

A 75-Year Connection

In the mid-1930's I was a teen-ager (although that term had not yet been invented), attending an all-girls secondary school. One interest which was actively encouraged was correspondence with pen-friends living in other countries. I volunteered enthusiastically to be put in touch with up to four correspondents.

I was soon in contact with Jessie, an American girl, Gerda in Germany, and two youths in what was then Czechoslovakia - Jaromir and Alex.

Some time before the outbreak of the Second World War Gerda wrote to tell me not to contact her again as she had joined the Hitler Youth Movement and regarded an English girl as an enemy.

Then I heard from Jaromir - known informally as Jaca - that his friend Alex had been drowned in a boating accident. By this time Jaca and I were conducting a kind of phantom romance by post. The photograph he had sent me showed an outstandingly beautiful young man. We seemed to have many interests in common, although his was a wealthy privileged Catholic background and mine anything but.

Once war had begun and Prague was distant in every respect, I had only Jessie as a pen friend. I had left school and my hopes of becoming a journalist had had to be placed in abeyance until life reverted to something like normal again.

During the early war years I worked in war-related jobs, followed by two and a half years in the Auxiliary Territorial Service, stationed at Bletchley Park. I had also by this time come to a kind of unacknowledged understanding with the man who would eventually become my husband. He had joined the RAF and went for bomber-pilot training to the United States. As Jessie and I were still in touch, I suggested that if his training commitments and the vast distance involved made it in any way possible, he might be able to contact her. To my delight, he managed to meet and talk with her, cementing our pen-friendship more firmly.

Shortly before my discharge from the ATS after the war ended, I was taking a short leave at my parent's house. Late one evening as I was preparing for bed there was a knock at my parents' front door, and when my mother opened it I was astonished to hear an unfamiliar voice saying "I am Jaromir Knittl from Czechoslovakia. Does Jean still live here?"

I did not go down in my dressing gown to meet him - my romantic foreign prince... My parents arranged overnight hospitality for him in the town and he returned the following morning.

We spent one whole day together, travelling to London and - because in his land locked country he had never walked on a sandy beach we went for a brief hour to the East Coast. Disappointingly, the shore was inaccessible because of the barbed wire and concrete barricades still in place against possible invasion.

We talked non-stop. His youthful beauty was no more - he had been actively involved in the Czech resistance, bore a scarred face and burnt hands, and looked at least twice his age. Of these experiences, he would not talk. We reminisced about our adolescent correspondence before acknowledging, with a little poignant regret, that our futures even as friends lay in very different directions.

He saw me onto my train at St. Pancras Station, kissed my hand in farewell and went to join some Czech refuges at a

London address he had brought with him. I no longer had an address for him in Prague and so never wrote to him again. A few months later I received a photograph showing him dressed in top-hat and morning suit, a stunningly beautiful blonde on his arm. They were approaching Prague Cathedral for their wedding. There was no accompanying letter.

Thus three of my four pen-friendships were ended.

Now to explain the 75-year connection.

Many years after all these youthful experiences, I received a letter telling me of Jessie's death. It was from her son, Guy, of whom she had written occasionally. He wrote of Jessie's serious ill-health (I could only imagine it was cancer) and that it had been decided to bring her home from hospital so that she could be with her family rather than "hooked up to a network of tubes and among strangers". Naturally, I wrote in sympathy, regretting that it was too late for me to say "Goodbye" to Jessie.

Then began a regular, if only at first at Christmas, contact with Guy, each of us exchanging briefly what was of importance in our lives, and our fears for the world. Our exchanges increased, and I learned of his period of ill health and recovery. That he continues to keep in touch on a regular basis I find touching - remarkable - and Jessie is the 75-year connection.

My Store-House

Fifty years - yes half a century
Since first this house became a home
So that each corner, every space - the very air
Holds vibrant memories.
Drawers and shelves weighted with mementos -
Programmes, letters, photos, greeting cards, books.

Once, parts of five lives were part of my own.
Two who still bring love and stories to add,
Two long since gone, but not beyond recall.
One who never could absorb the way of life
As lived in this home, left only regrets behind -
Disturbances in the constant passage
Of my remembrances, both glad and sad.
The other leaving me bereft, alone,
Haunts me hourly; now evoking smiles -
More often tears, grief scarcely to be borne.

So each day as I walk from room to room,
Adding to that vast memory store,
The gifts of freedom, precious friendships, music
I accept what was, is now, and still to come.

January 2010

On Survival - Lines on the Death of my Brother

The last living, loving link with the past is broken
And I am learning that survival
Has its own questions
Beyond those of bereavement -
Questions that demand response.

Is there now a role that I must play -
A guarantee against total forgetting -
Am I alone the one to ensure that those who come after
May learn their whole inheritance -
The flaws as well as the positives
Bestowed on them by our having lived?

Less weighty questions, too, tease the mind -
"Do you remember when...?"
"What happened to...?"
Such matters are not, in truth, so trivial
As it might seem,
Since to know the answers
Would confirm my place in our world -
A place that grows more fragile
With each passing, solitary day.

July 2010

Eulogy For My Brother

Yes, of course it comforts family and friends
Of the one they have lost
To hear, told aloud, the virtues and achievements.
But better by far, to tell while they live,
What they mean to you
And to the many touched by their life.

So this is for my brother,
As I want him and others
To know something of what he has been
And still is, for me.

We shared a childhood, true,
But six years, as well as gender, divided us then,
And for decades we scarcely met on any level.
Careers, the war, marriage, and physical distance
Ensured that meetings of mind and heart were rare -
Until, with the death of our parents, and our own ageing,
A gradual closeness began.

Now, after my widowing
And his virtual loss into her mental distance
Of his partner of sixty years
It appears that he and I share
More than physical siblinghood.

Of his achievement; his service,
His music, his career
I leave others to speak.
What I value
Is that we can talk of anything and everything.
And though we differ in some fundamentals
A mutual respect draws from each for the other
Warm recognition, new insight,
New understanding.

This, brother, is my eulogy for you
With my love.

Secret Communication

Hidden in a corner of memory
For more than half a century
Are thousands of stories
Once never to be told.
The oath of secrecy's
Now broken in books, films, television.

Long gone,
The multi-faceted diamond
That was Bletchley Park.
Flashing by day and night,
Passing vital details
To leaders of the Allied Forces

From the mighty Colossus computer
And the humbler red-lined paper sheets
That recorded coded radio intercepts
To be pored over conscientiously
In attempts to discover
The origins of each enigmatic message.

Now, seventy years on,
Those long-hidden stories
Have become simply tales to be told
Of communications no longer secret-

2012

I was one of Churchill's Geese

There are three versions of this account in Jean's writings, and although the time at Bletchley Park has been described in the Mingled Yarn manuscript, and in the Talk of The Town article, there are additional details here, as well as some duplication.

I felt that it was worth preserving this account too, and so I have amalgamated the three versions - Marianne

I was one of Churchill's Geese

I was born in Dunstable in 1921 and lived there with my parents and brother until I joined the ATS in September 1943. My father, Horace James Darby and my mother, Lilian Maud Darby (nee Sharrod), both came from large families, so there were many aunts, uncles and cousins around in various parts of London and the Home Counties.

My father was a partner in a hat factory in Luton. My mother worked in the home. When war broke out my father became a Captain in the Home Guard and my mother helped in a canteen for service personnel based in the town. She would often invite soldiers to our home for a meal and a hot bath, the latter being a luxury missed in their quarters. One of these service-men, a professional pianist in civilian life, treasured the odd opportunity to practise on our piano despite hands blistered and calloused from his duties in the Ordnance Corps.

My brother, a qualified surveyor, joined the Royal Engineers and I eventually went into the ATS (Auxiliary Territorial Service). This happened only after having begun training as a journalist on a local paper, the Harpenden Free Press, until 1939, when the proprietor who was a Major in the Territorial Army was called up and the paper was closed down. I then worked in a local office, and later as secretary to the Chief Engineer of what was then AC Spark Plug Company, where production had become fully geared to war-work. My boss was also a Home Guard Officer, in charge of the works' platoon, and between him and my father I found myself acting as clerk and 'runner' for the local 'Dad's Army'.

I began to want to feel more immediately involved in the war. I had changed from being a pacifist, and a member of the Peace Pledge Union to one who believed that unless Hitler was challenged and defeated, a greater evil even than modern warfare would threaten the free countries of the world. It was a hard decision to make in many ways, especially as a Christian and a lay preacher, but the atmosphere at the time, with the bombing of our cities and towns, and the news of Europe's sufferings were enough to convince me that I could make a contribution by joining one of the women's forces.

Then began a struggle with the War Office - which amazes me now when I remember the sort of letters I wrote to get myself released from a reserved occupation. I don't think I'd have the nerve today!

When I finally got permission to volunteer I tried first for the WRENs - attracted by the glamour of all things to do with the Navy and the sea. I was to discover just how elite the Senior Service can be! I was told that as I had no previous experience of anything to do with the sea, and no relatives ever having served with the Navy, my application would be rejected. Then I turned to the RAF. My current boy-friend was training to be a pilot and I had the romantic idea that if we were both wearing the same colour uniform it might keep us close! No luck there either. They only wanted clerks and I couldn't see the point of doing the same job as I was already for less money, away from home, and in uniform. Ah, the arrogance of youth! And where now was the patriotism?

So I turned to the ATS Auxiliary Territorial Service, now the women's Royal Army Corps. Here I had several tests, was told of the different sorts of service available and after the test results were examined it was suggested that I try for the intelligence corps, much to my amazement. (Not that I knew what that might involve.)

An interview followed in an underground bunker in Whitehall - very exciting! More questioning revealed that among my interests were crossword puzzles and the music of

J. S. Bach. This seemed to clinch matters and I was accepted for training.

Getting kitted out for ATS uniform had all of us involved both highly amused and slightly embarrassed. Extraordinarily designed heavy cotton bras, thick khaki knee-length elasticated knickers; were they called Victoria's? I remember my mother wearing this type. And pyjamas universally labelled passion-killers, heavy khaki lisle stockings, all very sensible no doubt, but not exactly romantic.

Initial training at a camp near Guildford lasted for three weeks. The normal period was six weeks, but either because we were understood to be "special" or they needed us in a hurry, our square-bashing period was minimal, much to the disgust and envy of those going on to other kinds of duties in the ATS.

Then it was off to London for signals training. I had no idea why I had to learn something called the radio Q-code and other technical details. At the end of this period, I was designated to be sent overseas, probably to North Africa. By this time, my mother was seriously ill following a major operation and I appealed to stay in the UK on compassionate grounds. This was granted, to my great relief, as I quickly succumb to extreme heat, and knew that Africa would be a difficult posting for me in every way.

All these preliminaries have been necessary for me to explain how it came about that I spent nearly two years at Bletchley Park. I had no idea what happened there, why I was sent, or what I was to become involved in.

Bletchley Park was to become for me, among much else, the higher education that I had never had, having left school at 15.

Arrival there was at once mundane and dramatic. We had travelled in the back of an Army truck, huddled uncomfortably on wooden seats with our kitbags on our knees. A command came from a regular Sergeant for us to form up in single file. Scrambling unaided and not very elegantly over the truck's tailboard we hastily recalled our Guildford training and tried to look as military as possible as we were marched towards a set of impressive gates and a sentry box manned by a red-capped military policeman.

I think, although I can't now be certain, that we had to give a password, - or perhaps it was just to show an official pass, and were then admitted to this extraordinary establishment. We'd all had to sign the Official Secrets Act which bound us never to reveal in our lifetime anything that we did, saw or heard here, otherwise we would suffer dire consequences. So that now so much has been written, filmed, and spoken of about Bletchley, it still seems strange to me that much of the work at the Park is in the public domain, as the saving goes, following the relaxing of the 30 year and 50 year rules regarding official secrets.

There is still a slight sense of unease, almost as though a dreadful fate still awaits any of us who talk! I have found others who seem to have forgotten a lot of detail - I had thought it was simply the forgetfulness of old age but there is an element I'm sure in me, as well as others, to deliberately forget certain things for this very reason - we can't then divulge anything we shouldn't.

For the first few weeks of my time at Bletchley Park, I was billeted in a private house in an outlying village, with a young woman whose husband was away in the Army; and who had a young child. My two chief memories of that time were the monotony of the rationed food, her staple evening meal for me was mashed potato on toast; and her favourite topic of

157

conversation which concerned mostly the physical details of her married life and childbirth. I was very naïve, and more of my innocence was quickly dispersed at that time.

My army pay, if I remember rightly was two shillings and sixpence a day (about 12½ pence - less than £1 a week) and of this, I arranged for half a crown to be sent home to my mother.

Once the Shenley Road Camp just outside the Park was completed, we were all accommodated in standard Army huts. As I remember, there were about 20 of us to each hut, sleeping on iron bedsteads with "biscuit" mattresses. These, for those of you who have never suffered them, consisted of three square cushions of hessian filled with straw, which in theory just fitted the bed frame. However, if they were slightly out of shape, or one was thicker than the other two, you can imagine that they were not a top of the range sleeping arrangement. In the centre of each hut was an iron stove, with a pipe going up through the ceiling and this had to be kept fed with coke and the ashes raked out night and day in cold weather - no-one's favourite task. There were small lockers for our clothes and other belongings, a shelf above the bed-space and that was it.

Bathing was an ordeal: what was known as the ablutions block, unheated, consisted of baths in brieze block cubicles, very small obscured windows and tiled floors. Each bath had a black line at 5" above the bottom of it and we were not supposed to fill the bath above that line. One officer recommended showers as an alternative to "stewing in our own juice!" I recall just one lovely bath-time when, from another cubicle I heard a glorious voice singing the bell song from Lakmé. The singer was a fellow ATS with whom I shared one or two musical experiences. Her first name was Joyce and I've often wondered whether she went on after the war to a professional career.

Another memory of the Camp is of dragging our beds out of the rear door of the hut and sleeping under the stars for a night, our oil skin groundsheets covering us against the cool damp of the dew.

The Commandant of the camp was a Colonel in the Greenjackets - which I believe was or is a Durham regiment. He was a stickler for military discipline, which didn't go down at all well with the types of people working in the Park. More of this man and his effect on us later, if there's time. But now to the Park itself, and what I knew at the time was happening there.

The security was amazing. There was such an atmosphere of respect for secrecy that one didn't know, and never attempted to find out what those in the next room were doing. You just got on with your own little task, having no inkling of where it came in the whole structure of code-breaking and recording of intelligence.

Indeed, until I returned a few years ago on a visit with Belper Travel Society I had not known at all what my part had been. I'll divert for a moment by explaining. As Bletchley Park is now open to the general public, I joined the party making this visit with a certain sense of both nostalgia and curiosity. When we arrived it seemed odd just to walk unchallenged through the main gates and then wander around at will. The main house itself, known in the war as The Mansion, was now open and equipped with various themed rooms.

During the time I was stationed there, the house was like a sacred temple. Only the very highest ranks were allowed inside, unless it was to attend an official lecture or meeting.

I set out to look for the hut where I had worked, but could not find it. I went into a small building where all the material from radio signalling work had been assembled, and had a chat with the volunteer manning the exhibition. He told me that my old block had been demolished but a replica had been built in another part of the park. I asked him a few questions, mentioning the red-lined pro forma I remembered, and learned that in fact I'd been working not on the famous Enigma coded messages, but another system called the Lorenz machine.

This had been intercepting wireless/teleprinter messages which those of us in a section code-named FISH studied to try to extract what we could. Sometimes the German operators might slip up and send part or all of a message in "clear", that is plain German, uncoded. If we saw this we got very excited and rushed the relevant slip of paper to our section leader to be passed up the chain. It was also possible to get some idea of coding as most messages began and ended with routine words, such as Heil Hitler and from that, one could perhaps work out other words in the message.

Incidentally, there was towards the end of the war a wireless intercepting outpost at Kedleston Hall. As the saying goes, - Not many people know that !

So now, after more than 70 years, I was learning a little of where I fitted in to that great enterprise.

This volunteer, in the course of our chat, said "So you were in the WRENS then?" This was yet another person who assumed all the brain-work done by women at Bletchley was by the WRENs. "No!" I protested vigorously. "I was in the ATS !" His response made me laugh. " Well, there were very few ATS working on that material. You are a very rare bird indeed."

See what I mean about the WRENs' apparent elitism? I may have forgotten some details of the day-to-day work, but remember nearly all the names of those I worked with and have vivid portraits of them in my mind, both what they looked like and their characters. The demands of the work, together with the intellectual standard of some colleagues meant that for me, it was a mind-stretching experience. So I have reason to be grateful for my time at Bletchley, as much for what happened off duty as my humble part in the war effort.

And the geese? Earlier in the war Churchill, on a visit to the Park, had made his famous remark that its workers were "the geese who laid the golden eggs for him," giving him the ammunition to fight the enemy effectively.

As I'm sure you know, there were many brilliant people working there, and there was every opportunity to mix with some of them on an equal footing both at work and leisure. At my level of course, I had no contact in working hours with the likes of the famous Alan Turing and other geniuses, but at meal times or in any of the countless off-duty activities you never knew who you'd be sitting next to. As well as the British there were individuals from all the allied nationalities engaged in the struggle - Poles, Free French and of course, later, when I was there, the glamorous Americans. They broke many hearts with their luxurious smart uniforms, their seemingly bottomless wallets, parcels from home and the breath of a free country which was home to Hollywood and all that signified to us film-goers at the time.

In our spare time there were chamber concerts (professional musicians to perform), drama groups (with professional actors), bridge clubs, sport of all kinds, madrigal societies, dancing - all tastes were catered for, including some of the less well-known religious groups such as the Christian Scientists.

(We had a young woman in our work-set who joined this group and refused all conventional medical help, even when suffering on one occasion from a wretched eye infection.) And there were men and women from every social group you could imagine - teachers, artists, civil servants, museum curators, journalists, librarians, business men, and of course the high academics. I could name drop here, but discretion forbids!

And so I learned a very great deal, not only in a number of new areas of knowledge, but about people, life, relationships and society. One example I remember - there was a certain Scotsman, a very pleasant individual most of the time, who nevertheless was sexist enough to maintain that we girls shouldn't have to do night shift - indeed shouldn't really be in the Forces at all. Our place was with the three Ks - Kitchen, Kirk and Kiddies. Just think what we said!

On another occasion I was chatting in our hut with a couple of my colleagues, one of whom was obviously from an upper-class background. At that time, I was sure that I didn't want to bring children into the world as it was then. Her response was: "Oh, but you are surely of good stock - healthy and intelligent. It's your duty to reproduce!"

I had a lot of fun too. When we were on night shift we ate in the officers' mess rather than the lower ranks' canteen, which closed at night. The food was a lot better and at the midnight meal break, if it was a fine night, we would go down to the lake, take out a rowing boat and circle the lake so disturbing the resident flock of Canada geese, which set up a cacophony of shrieks.

As well as activities in the Park's leisure programmes there were various things going on in the camp. I joined a play-reading group and on one occasion a visit from a female member of the royal family was expected, and the Colonel organised that a number of activities should be in progress to demonstrate how much he cared for our general well-being. For example, activities such as needlework, woodwork and table tennis. We chose to read a play (I can't remember its title) in which the line came, "Lo! yonder like a great balloon she comes" and we organised a signal that it should be proclaimed just as the princess was escorted through our hut door. It worked a treat.

Another of the Colonel's obsessions was meticulous smartness, for the camp and all who lived there. He would give a man sixpence to get his hair cut if he thought it half an inch too long, and when any important visitors were expected, he would get orderlies to paint the kerbs with white-wash and break off tree branches to stick in any bare patch of soil to look like a shrubbery.

My favourite spare-time activity was the main drama group. I can't think how we managed the elaborate costumes for "Berkeley Square" - a play set in two different time sequences, one of them needing 18th century dress. But, we did it, and there are some photographs to prove it!

Returning for a moment to night-shifts - there was a hut set aside for those needing to sleep in the daytime. It was relatively quiet, away from the main part of the camp, but there was no way of making it really dark. And - this may be a bit embarrassing - to shut out the light we devised a cunning strategy. This was in the days of looped sanitary towels, and we used to fix the loops over our ears so that the bulk of the towel acted as a muffler over our eyes. Crude, but effective!

The last days of my time at Bletchley were strange. The Germans were in retreat and what messages were being sent were mostly uncoded and were sometimes hardly readable, with long gaps. As the traffic I was mostly concerned with was from German HQ to the Generals, or vice versa, this was a time of great confusion. We sat around a lot, I remember, waiting for something to report.

Eventually the inhabitants of the Park began to say their goodbyes, except that is for those who had found romance during their time there, and there were quite a number of those.

I was posted to an Army depot in Nottingham and because I had a Sergeant's stripes I was expected to do some drill duty on occasion, much to my dismay. I'd forgotten everything I'd ever learned at Guildford. On one never-to-be-lived-down occasion I was trying to drill a platoon, got them marching successfully but in a fairly confined space. As they headed towards a solid brick wall I realised that I hadn't the faintest idea how to turn them round. You can picture the ensuing chaos!

On demobilisation from the ATS, after our many separations and other relationships, I'm happy to report that I eventually I married David Sealey, the blue-uniformed RAF pilot of my pre-Bletchley days who had flown Halifax bombers during the last three years of the war. My wedding dress was home-made from Nottingham lace, the coupon ration not stretching to anything more elaborate.

FISHES OF
BRITAIN'S RIVERS AND LAKES

by
J. R. NORMAN
*Assistant Keeper, British Museum
(Natural History)*

The KING PENGUIN *Books*
PUBLISHED BY PENGUIN BOOKS LIMITED
LONDON *and* NEW YORK
1943

Signatures of all members of "Fish Section", Bletchley Park, 1945. Head of Section David Uzielli (later changed name to ?Hutchinson)

See also second "page" from flyleaf of book "Fishes of Britain's Rivers and Lakes

Drama productions at Bletchley Park

During my time at Bletchley Park, drama, as well as other artistic activities, flourished. There were groups in both the park itself and in Shenley Road Military camp.

I was personally involved in one way or another with productions of Bernard Shaw's 'Candida', J.B. Priestley's 'They Came To A City' and an ambitious presentation of 'Berkeley Square'. I wish I could recall how we managed all the professional costumes for this play, which is set in two time periods, requiring several changes.

A close friend, Jeanne Cammaerts, daughter of Emile Cammaerts, was also active in drama events and staged T.S. Eliot's 'Family Reunion'. In addition to productions there was also a lively play- reading group.

Production of "Berkley Square" Bletchley Park 1945

Shenley Road Military Camp
Drama Group

Berkeley Square

ASSEMBLY HALL
—Wilton Avenue—

March 13th & 14th, 1945

PROCEEDS TO THE
ARMY BENEVOLENT FUND

Programme 3d.

Fisher & Sons, Printers, Woburn

BERKELEY SQUARE
— BY —
J. L. BALDERSTON and J. C. SQUIRE.

Characters in order of appearance.

Maid	... L/Cpl DOROTHY SAYER
Tom Pettigrew	L/Cpl ALASTAIR WALLIS-NORTON
Miss Pettigrew	S/Sgt. MARGARET BURNHAM
The Lady Anne Pettigrew	S/Sgt. LOIS FOSTER-CARTER
Mr. Throstle	L/Cpl. DOUGLAS KEYTE
Helen Pettigrew	Sgt. IRIS GARGERY
The Ambassador	L/Cpl. IAN TAYLOR
Mrs. Barwick	Sgt. ELAINE DEACON
Peter Standish	Sgt. DEREK DAVIES
Marjorie Frant	Sgt. ANNE BOURNE
Major Clinton	Sgt. DESMOND MASON
The Duchess of Devonshire	Sgt. BETTY HICKMAN

Scene : The morning room of a Queen Anne House
in Berkeley Square.

ACT I.—Scene 1. Five o'clock October 23rd, 1784.
Scene 2. Five o'clock October 23rd, 1928.
Scene 3. Continuous with Scene 1, 1784.

ACT II.—Night, a few days later, 1784.

ACT III. Scene 1. Afternoon, a few weeks later, 1784.
Scene 2. Continuous with Scene 1, but in 1928.

THE PLAY produced by Cpl. JEAN DARBY.

Stage Manager ... Sgt. LESLEY STUART TAYLOR
Production Secretary ... Sgt. JOHN THOMPSON
Lighting ... LESLIE EDWARDS
Scenery ... L/Cpl. CECIL WALLER
House Manager ... Sgt. HENRY BALEN

Costumes and Wigs by
H. & M. RAYNE and B. J. SIMMONS.

There will be two intervals of ten minutes.

The Committee wishes to express its grateful thanks to
all who have given their kind help and co-operation.

The French Group will produce MARIUS
— in May —

THE PLAY produced by Cpl. JEAN DARBY

Production of "Berkley Square" Bletchley Park 1945

170

Feb 21-25 1944 "Candida"

Production of "Candida (G.B. Shaw)
Bletchley Park Dramatic Society 1944

B.P. DRAMA GROUP

THEY CAME
TO A CITY

By J. B. PRIESTLEY

In aid of the SOLDIERS', SAILORS' and AIRMEN'S FAMILIES FUND

*There will be no admission to the auditorium
when the curtain has risen*

Price 3d.

THEY CAME TO A CITY

A Play in Two Acts

By J. B. PRIESTLEY

CAST

JOE DINMORE	MALCOLM HOWGATE
MALCOLM STRITTON	RICHARD BRIGHT
CUDWORTH	DOUGLAS JONES
SIR GEORGE GEDNEY	ERIN NEWTON-JOHN
ALICE FOSTER	PAMELA GIBSON
PHILLIPA LOXFIELD	VERA NAISMITH
LADY LOXFIELD	SHIRLEY RHODES
DOROTHY STRITTON	CHRISTINA KNOWLES
MRS. BATLEY	JEAN DARBY

Produced by PETER LABERTOUCHE

The action takes place during one day outside a strange city.

(To prevent damage to the floor the audience is asked NOT TO SMOKE in the auditorium)

Stage Manager	EDNA OWEN
Wardrobe Mistress	EVELYN HILL
Lighting	DUDLEY OWEN AND MONTAGUE WARD
Set Built and Painted by	JOHN LOWE AND ROY BOOKER, *assisted by* KENNETH GILSON
Production Secretary	MARJORIE MATTHEWS
Business Manager	REGINALD PARKER
Stage Assistants	JOHN HARRISON AND RICHARD PENDERED

Material for the set kindly lent by
BLETCHLEY CO-OPERATIVE SOCIETY

Next Production :

IBSEN'S
ROSMERSHOLM

Produced by PENELOPE STOREY

November 16, 17, 18 and 20

"They Came to a City" programme
Mrs Batley played by Jean Darby

173

The Commemorative Badge

BLETCHLEY PARK
National Codes Centre

70 YEARS
HOME OF THE
CODEBREAKERS
BLETCHLEY
PARK 1939-2009

Thank you for contacting us concerning the announcement by the government of a commemorative badge for veterans who worked at Bletchley Park or one of its Outstations during WWII.

Please find enclosed the form for you to apply for the Government recognition commemorative badge. Once completed this form needs to be return to GCHQ. The address for this is on the form.

If you would also like to apply for Freedom of Bletchley Park. Please complete the enclosed green & purple forms and return to Bletchley Park. The address is on the bottom of the form.

THE GOVERNMENT CODE AND CYPHER SCHOOL

Jean Sealey

The Government wishes to express
to you its deepest gratitude
for the vital service you performed
during World War II

Gordon Brown

Rt Hon Gordon Brown MP
Prime Minister

July 2009

The Height of Hypocrisy

They've remembered us all with a medal -
- A little gilt brooch with a pin
And a little blue stone in the middle
And a thank you note from the P.M.

It's sixty years since we were demobbed.
Why now would they make such a move,
When most of the thousands who worked there
Have long since left all life and love?

There's been a half-hearted apology
For the treatment of the Park's brightest brain.
I wonder where they sent HIS medal?
Or whether it was best to refrain.

Is it all of a piece with the present?
There's the latest memorial stone
To the RAF's thousands of heroes,
And those who never came home.

Will the world never learn the stark lesson?
Even now Afghanistan and Iraq
Send hundreds of flag-draped coffins
To the mourning families in black.

Poetry with Punch

In 2007 Jean, together with Alec Rapkin and Jeremy Duffield, was one of the featured poets at a 'Poetry with Punch' annual event organised by Cathy Grindrod and Christine Davies.

In 2014 a book was published by WordWork Press called Poetry With Punch, and it is a collection of poems and memories of the poets involved in the events over the previous fifteen years. This is Jean's 2014 'memory' of the event in 2007:

> **Poetry with Punch Remembered:**
> I remember what a delightful occasion it was. At 92 I'm now partially sighted and shakily mobile but I'm still very interested in poetry matters and wish the coming events every success. **Jean**

Jean contributed this poem which she wrote in 2011 to the book:

No Traveller Returns

As hidden brooklets
Quiet streams
And mighty gushing rivers
All seek the boundless oceans,
So each of our disparate lives
Must find its unique way
To that unknown afterwards.
Now across sunlit meadows -
Now through tunnels of grief
Or round boulders of disbelief.
There can be no damming of the waters -
Only an acceptance that there may be
An Afterwards.

Well, Jean, we can't leave it there can we? One last set of poems, and thank you for all you have shared.

Haiku Sequence

Falling golden leaves
Currency from Nature's mint
Income for bonfire.

Bonfire smoke rising
Blown by sudden gust of wind
Brings tears for year's death.

Year dying night frosts
Following bright golden days
Confirm autumn's hold.

As petals float down
From dying passion-flowers
Past loves fade slowly.

Autumn trees aflame
Burning through soft falling rain
Rekindle lost hopes.

Clear eyes of infants -
Like smooth waters of the lake -
Reflect cloudless sky.

A banana skin
Waits on the path of the man
Who turns up his nose.

Printed in Great Britain
by Amazon